# Promise Me

Wayne Mckillop

# People

Betty is the mother who is HIV+

Harry is Betty's ex, and our Father, he lives in McKinney, TX.

Big Mike is Betty's boyfriend and is HIV+, they live in Plano, TX.

Linda is the oldest and lives in Denver, Co.

Laurie lives in Kansas City, MI

Jeff lives in Austin, TX

I'm Wayne, and I live in Denver with my wife, Jenny and daughters Ryan and Tessa.

Ally lives in Plano with her kids, Corey, Zach, and Lauren

Tracy lives in Dallas with her husband Dan and kids Nick, Big Ben, Daniel, Spike, and Emma.

# CONTENTS

# About the Author

'There's really not too much to say about myself.  I'm probably a pretty regular, normal guy. Have done the same things we all do. I was out the other night and a friend read my 'About the Author' and she said "you are so much more than this." I think we all are. We each are so much more than what people see.  She said "write about being a teacher, a father and a friend." And I have.

This story took place 30 years ago.  As I look back, I'm not sure how much I have changed.  It's like we are born as we are and we experience many things, some magnificent things beyond our imagination. These experiences may alter or change our being only this much.  The rest we stay as we are.  Our experiences don't define us, we define our experiences.

# Introduction

This is a true story.

I did add a couple things about my daughter, Jane, she wasn't alive yet, but she wanted to be in a book. I added her 3 times, once at a birthday party, once when she was on the edge and once in a black box. And I added Max's name a couple times.

I also added a couple things about Harry because he did amazing things.

And, I added a love letter from Julie dated 1996. I added it because things get better.

The rest is all true.

The story is letters I wrote to Jenny, a wife, and from a journal.

It's a story about the things we do. A story about the people we love.

Ultimately, it's a story about Betty. Her living and dying. It's filled with love, joy, pain and suffering.

And it's a story about her death.

Words define and limit an experience.

Some of this stuff was beyond the words.

Page Blank Intentionally

# Chapter 1

*Thursday, January, 9th, 1993*

*Dear Jenny,*

*How are you?*

*I just took off from Denver on my way to Dallas. It was cool. I could see the north side of Wash Park and looked for you and the kids. I have spent most of the flight looking out the window, searching for something. I couldn't find anything that made sense of what I'm doing.*

*It seems like all I will find will be what is right before me; no searching will be needed. It will be right there, yet there is no telling what it will look like, each time it arises it may look different, which seems wild. Right? I don't know.*

*I'll miss you. Leaving something, someone, you see it behind you, and it looks different. You've always looked good from the front and the behind.*

*The flight was good, but I was hungry, and they gave us peanuts. Two guys were hitting on a lady; I don't know if she knew, she was thinking she was making a sale or a contact. I don't know, maybe.*

*I have to find somewhere to begin when I get to Dallas.*

*I have got to go. Take care. I love you.*

### *Thursday late night*

*Billy picked me up from the airport last night and drove me to Baylor Hospital to see Betty. It was 730pm when I walked into room 717. I felt blinded by the darkness of the room. I flipped on a small orange night light, and there she was, Betty, tucked into bed like a child, sleeping soundly, peacefully. I stood quietly with crashing waves of thoughts and emotions sweeping over me. Some were deep stabs of fear and sadness; others were gentle and loving. It was as if that was necessary. Betty opened her eyes, eyes you could look into forever, and with a gentle smile, she told me everything would be all right. We seemed motionless, looking at each other, our eyes revealing our hearts. I swear it felt right then that everything would be okay, things would work out. I sank into a chair, and we continued our assurances, talking about things that had always meant so much, and these things came alive once again; you could smell Christmas and taste Slim Jims and Heath bar. We remembered when I ran out of 1st grade and into her arms, arms I want to hold now. Arms wrapped around me, being held together by love. How many times will that happen?*

*It was all wonderful, once in a lifetime, to be there. And then there was a loud knock on the door. It was the police, and suddenly the calm was shattered and we were jolted roughly back into the darkness of the night. The police asked who I was and what I was doing here, and a fleeting glimmer of hope passed; maybe Betty and I weren't supposed to be here. I told them who I was, it wasn't much. They said they detained Billy. Billy, oh no. While in another space with Betty, I forgot about Billy. Billy had been walking around, wandering, checking the hospital out for the past 2 hours, and it was late, so nurses had called for backup, and here we were.*

*Billy is how he is. He can manifest what the rest of us dream of. He's different. He's lived different lives during his lifetime. He can talk to people who are no longer there and be in places that aren't real. Maybe the people and places were real long ago, even if they never were, Billy was there. We all go there or we want to go there, where our head or heart changes our reality. Billy's there a lot; say his percentage of the time is this much, mine would be an amount of time too, I don't know. So Billy walking the hospital halls could have been a med vac in a war or a natural disaster; he's been everywhere. I understood the nurses' concern, they didn't want to turn the hospital into a war zone. The officers asked a few more questions about people, places, planes, trains, and automobiles, our stories matched closely enough. They advised us that visiting hours were over and then thanked Billy for his service! It was unreal, right? What if Billy's world is the real world?*

*Shortly after, I kissed Betty goodnight, and Billy and I left.*

*The night was young, "Wild Billy shook some dust out of his coon skin hat," he said. "Wayne, try some of this, it will show you where it's at or at least help you through it," Bruce Springsteen, 'Spirit in the Night.'*

*We got on top and headed to a Mexican restaurant, a favorite of Billy's. The owner, waiters, waitresses, and bartenders knew Billy, knew his order and brought him his drink; it all happened without a word. They loved Billy and thanked him for whatever he did for them. There was tons of food and drink, it was a delicious, fantastic night, a bit unreal.*

# Chapter 2

*Friday, January 10th, 1992*

*Dear Jenny,*

*How are you?*

*It's not bad here. It's a slow morning, and I'm clearing my head from last night. I had a big late breakfast, two sausages (.74), browns (.48), two eggs (.62), biscuit and gravy (.33), and toast (.8), so that has helped. It seems like someone worked hard to come up with those prices. It is now later in the afternoon. Ally is working, and Tracy was here earlier.*

*I have to do something, figure something out, and make a plan. I don't know probably anything about AIDS, I've heard about it, have known it's been around for a few years, and constantly stayed away from it. It is not something that is being embraced, people want it contained, 'keep it there, not here,' not near me." Something so far away, something you would never think could be real, then can become real life so quickly, and for it to carve out such a massive part in your life. What exactly is HIV? How do you live with HIV?*

*Betty has a doctor who treats people who are HIV+. Dr. Steven Pounders. Dr. Pounders has an AIDS clinic, CCC, that Betty goes to for treatment. Betty and Tracy love him.*

*Hear what that means, "Thank you so much for the care from your heart?" Healing and caring. This area of Betty's care is in good hands. Some people are caring for Betty who care for her.*

*Maybe I'll look at her finances, insurance, money, how she pays for stuff, and what about her nursing job; the hospital doesn't know that Betty is HIV+. That's a bit wild, what are they going to do? You can't have a nurse with AIDS. Where was Betty infected with HIV? There is probably enough stuff here to keep me busy and move us forward.*

*I don't know what this disease will do to Betty. What about the loss? How do you lose Betty? I can't come close to this, why or how do we jump to the end so quickly. It overwhelms the fibers of your life. Betty is still a young soul; she is so beautiful.*

*'You believe in the Father, the Son, and the holy*

*ghost,' whose hands is Betty's life in? It's got to be all those around her.*

*It's not time for this.*

*Later,*

*I called Dale. Dale is a nurse at the clinic Betty goes to, CCC, Comprehensive Care Clinic. Dale loves Betty, and I believe that. There's a lot of love. Dale is a good person, how can you be so good? He gave me a direction that cut to the chase: a lawyer, housekeeping, rides, groups, meals, places to get drugs and medication, lots of support, lots of caring. It's another world inside the world; there are probably thousands of people living beyond the news, living in their world of pain, suffering, and dying, and among them are all of us.*

*Betty is weaker than I would have thought. She can barely walk, not very far, only to the end of the room. She can't attend to herself, she can't care for herself. This may be how it will go: times of being comfortable and interacting getting shorter, and times of discomfort, pain, indignity, or suffering, these times get longer. Betty will be here for another week when she may feel slightly better. It takes time to recover from the depths she goes to, and it takes time for her body to adjust to medication being pumped into her, fed to her, medication only made to slow down the dying. Really, that sounds backward. There is no cure for HIV, nothing to stop it. Do you know what HIV does to your body? Right now, it does this, this is what her mouth looks like while sleeping, it's drawn down, reaching as far as it can into sadness, even in her sleep, she is sad. HIV begins with sorrow and progresses.*

*I need to go, I need to run, I need to sleep, I need to dream.*

*I love you.*

# Chapter 3

*Saturday, January 11th, 1992*

*Hey Jenny,*

*How are you now? Some of it's been tough without me, uh?*

*I haven't gotten very far; it seems like I set out to do something or find something, and I go in a circle and end up right where I started. Maybe it's not a circle, it's a dead end. And there seem to be so many situations. They're endless, everything is new, there are frustrations and letdowns, and as soon as you start with something, something else comes up and bites hard, it's unbelievable, gotta go.*

*Hello. I'm back in Betty's room. She just finished with an MRI. We were there for a while, the doctors wanted to look at her liver. Baylor is a teaching hospital. With teaching there is learning; many student doctors and student nurses follow the leader, the teacher, and each patient is their classroom. And they test everything, which doesn't necessarily lead to an answer but rules out stuff, and then they think they know, seemingly backward. And they all know Betty is HIV+, and to different degrees they aren't necessarily comfortable, HIV is scary. You can see 5-6-7 doctors come into the room, just inside the doorway, that's as close as they want to be. Right before they wheeled Betty to the MRI, she got sick to her stomach, and there it is, HIV, you can see it. The HIV, its right there, something can kill you is right there. Who's going to touch it? Who's going to get close to Betty? You could reach out. She gets sick, and it is hard for her to eat or do anything. She had a spoonful of soup, and it made her ill. Look how little a spoonful is, she can't keep anything down. Are you serious? How does this work?*

*Later,*

*I've been here since 930 this morning, and now my favorite part of the day is coming up at 5 p.m. every day hundreds and hundreds, in massive clusters, swallows fly through the sky outside the window, up and down everyday they go, back and forth they go, every day they go.*

*Love forever, Wayne.*

# Chapter 4

*Sunday, January 12th, 1992*

*Dear Jenny,*

*Geez, I don't know what to say. I've often had these dreams where everything around me starts to inflate, to grow into these vast, overwhelming beings or things, and they smash up into me over and over again, and they squeeze and squeeze the life out of me. They're the things we deal with in our lives, things left undone, promises broken, money things, relationship things, and now all these things are here.*

*Right after I arrived at the hospital this morning, they knocked Betty out for the next 3 hours. This is how they treat her pain and nausea, they send her to another planet because they can't treat her here. They can't treat her because they're unsure what causes her to be sick, so they zap her way out there and hope it goes away, and her. I spoke with a nurse and she didn't know too much. She told me I needed a doctor, and I told her I didn't. You're out there, and it is sometimes hard to find a way back.*

*You should hear the patient in the next room, a nurse just told her to be quiet. The patient is a very old woman, small, frail, bony, she's crumbled over, gnarled into a ball and she wails and wails like a hoarse baby, a baby that has become an older adult. She wails for something that will soothe her, a touch, a hug, like a baby. Another nurse just went by, mumbling under her breath that she didn't 'have the time' to deal with the wailer in the next room.*

*I'm not sure what floor we are on, but all the patients seem to be at the end of life. They all seem to be dying. When I walk by, glance in a room, they are lying in bed, their eyes are closed, their skin looks like it was placed over bones, it's a pale darkish white color, how white is just before it becomes black, how life becomes death, and their mouths are open, life coming in and life going out. Everything is quiet. Imagine. Put your loved one there.*

*I looked over at Betty, she's still alive, she's asleep, she looks good, her color is good. Her mouth is closed reaching down to her chin. She's sad and scared. She probably can't believe it, how do you manage? How do you live with a terminal disease without always dying?*

*The nurses are here, Betty is crying from pain, it hurts so much it makes her cry. They had to start an IV in her arm, and they were having a hard time, trying time after time to find a vein, and each time it hurt more and more. Then they had to remove a medication port that was inserted in her chest. The line in the port is infected, and they think that is causing her to get sick. But they don't know, 'we'll find out.' There are complications, and there is the unknown, they may not know enough about AIDS, and Betty is female, and there don't seem to be a lot of HIV females. This is happening everywhere, people caring for people dying.*

*Betty isn't that well. She doesn't eat, she can't get out of bed, she hurts, she cries, the bad things block out a lot, and you are left with maybe just a tiny glimmer of light to lead you out of the darkness. It's hard, and sometimes it seems you're not going to make it out, but as long as there is something, there will be some light in her life.*

*I don't know. Right now, there is no good news or positive news; 'look for the positive.' I don't want to, any settling or calm you find, results from being in the terribleness and then being in the peacefulness. The wailer is awake and crying out, and the lady visiting tells her to 'shut up.' Like, just shut up and die. We've already moved on, and you are forgotten!*

*I guess you call upon whatever you have, whatever you believe in, and whatever may help you whenever there is only a glimmer. I'm sitting in an empty hallway with comfortable chairs, looking outside. I can hear the wailer; the sky outside is overcast, dark, and dreary, and it looks like rain, and I wonder and wonder.*

*Later,*

*We did get some good news. The MRI returned, and the liver is good, with just a bit of tissue deposit; the same with the lymph nodes; they are also okay. The doctor said they are looking for cancer. With HIV, there is a higher possibility of cancer. He explained that Betty has CMV, an infection that can spread through her body and damage the organs. People might have CMV, but we have T-cells, white blood cells that attack and stop CMV and infections. HIV is a virus that destroys T-cells; it destroys white blood cells, and as our T-cells are destroyed, the body cannot fight off the infections that will ravage the body and organs from the inside out. Betty has CMV on an ulcer on her esophagus.*

*After his prognosis, Betty asked in a quiet voice, almost a whisper, "How long?"*

*How long is life is the shortest way there is?*

*Hello,*

*It's later, I don't know, I can't get my brain to think, I can't focus, I can't have a thought. All I do is feel. It's not one emotion; it is 2-3-4 different emotions. The dark ones, fear, anger, sadness, and they come to you all at once, you get all mixed up and confused about what you are feeling and you start to feel absolute madness. What do you do in your madness? What do you do when things around you are out of the norm? When madness becomes the norm, what do you do when madness, depression, and fear settle inside you? It's crazy. It's like our bodies and our being are made to deal and interact with just so much and beyond that; we may get sick, we may get broken, we may hurt. When our bodies get so broken, they wear down, they're depleted, they stop. When our being gets so broken, so hurt, so broken from the pain and the sadness, it stops being and you're wracked by madness and depression till you find your way. And how do you do that? I'll tell you, it's a long story.*

*Hello, sitting, it's been a couple of hours. Betty will open her eyes, look around, and slowly close her eyes. I don't think she sleeps, she closes her eyes not to see what is out there.*

*Take care, I love you,*
*Wayne*

# **Chapter 5**

*Monday, January 13th, 1992*

*Dear Jenny,*

*How's it going?*

*It sounds like you guys are getting some snow and bad weather. I hope you guys stay safe and warm. It was official that at 9:00 a.m., Monday, January 13th, 1992, we had an "essential appointment" with Holly Wesebaum, BSW, Social Worker 1. I don't know if it was Holly Wesbaum, BSW, Social Worker 1's very bright aqua blue dress, or, was it when Holly asked Betty if she was "having a nice day?" but golly, there is stuff around you to pay attention to, and Holly was rolling along with her training and personality that didn't read this room. You know many people out there want to help; some may, some may not, and we will cross paths with many people and added all together they are very knowledgeable, caring, and competent.*

*Last night was such a drag. It was late; I was dying to get out of the hospital and couldn't. First, I got lost in the hospital while trying to get out. Baylor is an old hospital, and they have added more buildings and more facilities and many more hallways to connect everything. They ended up with long underground hallways, and the hallways are so long, where they end looks so small. All the hallways lead to four major intersections, each with a bronze bust of who the building was named after. At each of the four intersections are four hallways that rip off in another direction, 4 x 4 = 16 different hallways, one of which I was looking for. I got lost. I could have looked at the map, but who does that? I wandered, searching for a way out, finding no way out. 'Wasted and I can't find my way home' Blind Faith*

*I asked someone, an old man, not sure what he was doing, "How do I get to the parking garage?"*

*"Which one?"*

*"Don't know."*

*"Well," he said, "You have to know where you're going to get to where you want to be."*

*That was it. I need to figure out where I'm going. I got there, tired, frustrated and when I found the car, there was a parking ticket on the car, ok, no sweat. I started home and ran out of gas at the exit before mine. Betty's car is a Mercedes that Harry bought her to win her back, and the Mercedes is a diesel. But it seems that whatever was fucking with me got tired because 100 yards away was a gas station with a gas can and diesel. I got home, exhausted and crashed, knowing I had to return at 9 a.m. for an essential meeting with Holly Wesenbaum, BSW, Social Worker 1.*

*Have a good day today Jenny,*
*I love you.*

# Chapter 6

*Tuesday, January 14th, 1992*

*Hello Jenny,*

*It is Tuesday, about 3:30 p.m., and time goes by fast when you are just sitting around.*

*I spoke with an attorney yesterday on the phone and then went down to see him. I thought he would have experience and know what was going on legally about some issues. But he didn't say or do anything that indicated that he knew anything. He was not a trial lawyer, and he didn't seem to be knowledgeable about issues or HIV or anything. He knew nothing of recent lawsuits or settlements. And he bothered me, horrified me with his absolute insistence "that HIV is transmitted only one way, and that way is through anal sex," and he said there was no way Betty could have contracted HIV any other way. Fuck you asshole. "Not through her work at the hospital, not any other way." Shut the fuck up.*

*I don't know, the purpose of an attorney is to see how*

*Betty gets what she needs: medical attention and care. We won't know about many things until they happen, and we have to be ready as best we can.*

*At this point Betty has a large stack of medical bills to pay. Her option at this point is to go on long-term disability, 70% of her income; she pays her medical premiums and the deductible, which would then net her less than 50% of her income. This does not sound like enough. We are looking for more money and maybe something from the hospital to support this. What about Presbyterian Hospital, where she worked? We don't even know where she contracted HIV.*

*Anyway, the lawyer was a big zero, so we decided that I would go to Presbyterian and tell someone that Betty is HIV+, that she may not be able to work at the hospital, she may have to quit.*

*Betty doesn't know where she contracted AIDS. She said she had a short affair with a doctor ten years ago during Harry's divorce. Betty and others say that Big Mike may have infected her, that Big Mike has a lifestyle that includes others. If that's the case, I want to kill you, almost maybe. You must have known, why did you do it? Why did you? Fuck.*

*So there are a lot of things that go on and many more thoughts that go on, and you lay there with them, and they swirl around and get bigger and bigger until they aren't just bothersome, they are incredibly overwhelming, complicated, and maddening. Everything seems so extreme.*

*As far as Betty's health goes, she's doing pretty well today. She was awake this morning for about 2 to 3 hours. She didn't get out of bed, but she was awake and knows what was happening around her. Tracy's kids visited. They light up Betty's life. She is so happy to see them, so pleased for the hugs and stories they tell. Betty loves them beyond. A love that happens how many times in your life? She sees their happiness and feels her own, she sees their child's life and it gives her life, she feels alive around the grand kids. And their love for her is the same back. It's like it was blessed.*

*Health wise, there's medicine to stop pain and suffering. There is no medicine to stop HIV. There is no cure, there is no stopping HIV. Betty had an ultrasound today, they are still looking at the liver. At one point they said the liver was okay. So we sat around and waited to hear about that today. They are also examining her heart and the artery above the heart for a clot or murmur. Besides these three things that they continue to test, there is also concern about an infection somewhere that causes her to be constantly nauseous. So we sit and wait, and it all looks something like this:*

*Ulcer  - being treated*          *Heart - testing*

*Nausea -being treated*        *Artery -testing*

*Infection - being treated*

*And the financial stuff:*

*Medical bills - growing*          *Future cost/expenses - don't know*

*Go to Presbyterian on Thursday*

*And this stuff:*

*Home care?*                 *Medication?*

*Diet?*            *Support?*

*Other?*

*And it continues. We're trying to find out about support groups and AIDS groups that maybe Betty would want to do. I also need to finish painting Betty's bedroom and maybe get support bars in her bathroom.*

*Some things are happening and getting done, but it is all so slow, and getting something done leads to 3-4 more things to do.*

*How are things in Denver?*

*I miss Denver, my house, my room, my stereo, my kids, my life, and my wife.*

*Take care,*

*I love you,*

*Wayne*

# Chapter 7

*Wednesday, January 15th, 1992*

*Hey Jenny,*

*Another day, another hallway, another test, we're sitting, waiting in a hallway in nuclear medicine, like there is such a thing.*

*Betty just had a third test on her liver, and after we wait one more hour in the hallway, she will have a fourth test done on the liver. Medicine is crazy. Maybe it's the HIV that they aren't as proficient in. Betty is HIV, and HIV spreads out from Betty, out from her room, and people don't want it. It's weird. And it's frustrating to take four tests and not know the answer, and then all we can do is sit and wait in the hallway and try to make Betty comfortable as she lays on a hospital stretcher in a hallway.*

*Goodbye.*

# Chapter 8

*Jenny, Jenny, Jenny,*

*How are you?*

*At this moment, I have forgotten all but the best of us. It must be the frivolousness of life that I often pay attention to and then get hung up on the little things that happen that should pass me by. Those are the things that I need not pay attention to. How is it that? Maybe it's a warning, a marriage defined by who does the dishes or folds shit the right way. If folding clothes establishes the marriage, where does it go? And right now, all those things are forgotten, and I intensely love you. Love is how I love you.*

*I have been here for about a week now. Today is Thursday, about 3:45 p.m., which always seems to be the same time. I've been in the hospital for seven days, and I don't feel any better. It's not so much being here. Part of it is wondering what I'm not doing or what I used to do that I now don't do. It's like I was lifted right out of my life and it still goes on without me. How can you not be a part of your life?*

*And meanwhile, I'm here, I guess a new part of my life. The hospital is good. The nurses are getting to know us, and they become a little nicer as they get to know Betty. Since she's been here, they've seen her family and her life, and that's who she becomes and how they treat her. I'm not sure how long Betty will be here. My last estimate last Sunday was that she would be here for 6 or 7 more days, today's Wednesday. Maybe sometime this weekend Betty will be ready to leave, two or three days more sounds right.*

*As I wrote the above line, one of the student doctors came in. Betty was asleep so we went into the hallway to talk. The doctor said that Betty would be released tomorrow on Thursday. I was shocked. Yesterday Betty had four tests done, two on her liver and two on her heart, and she was unable to eat all day long. This morning she had minor surgery to implant an IV line below her shoulder, and she still hasn't been able to eat, she cannot walk on her own, she has vomited all morning. She is currently zonked way out there in a different space and now in my space a happy doctor is smiling, telling me that Betty is ready to go home. I flipped out and grabbed the doctor by the neck, took her to the ground, started choking her, and watched her turn blue. Can you imagine? There's a madness to all this. and it can flip you. And how do you release it the anger, the fear? It felt defeating. We were here for something, here to get better. Here to know why Berry was sick and we haven't gotten what we came for. I was scared of everything. And we were to take care of Betty. How do you do that?*

*I asked the doctor what they had done to improve anything. She chuckled and said they were sending Betty home with the longest list of medicines. I thought, bullshit, grabbed her by the neck… I asked the doctor to wait, I wanted to talk to Dr. Pounders to see what he thinks. We don't know the answers to too many unanswered questions. She chuckled again. What the fuck is wrong with her? Why is she chuckling again and walking away? It all seemed so unreal. I thought Betty would be healthier when she left than when she got here; that's not the case, and it's hard to understand. What was she here for? What have they done for her? Did they make her better? Can anyone hear the screaming? The deep, dark screams inside of you, the screams that no one can hear, have you had those? Have you heard them? I don't know. Someone has to be able to do something. If you hear screaming or crying, do something, do what you can, touch someone with your heart.*

*What a day! It is a little later, and I'm sitting in Betty's room while she sleeps. I've been thinking about the hospital and how they help people. The wailer was gone this morning; there is no way that old women could have been released. Where is she now? There was also a girl who was slowly pushing her brother out. He was so thin; she was pushing bones sticking out under the skin, with no color, paleness, white with no color, and wisps of hair- so few that you could count them. He had an IV pole that was keeping him alive, and they were leaving. How could they be able to leave? Where do they go? Who cares for him? And you won't believe this other guy two doors down. Yesterday was his first day here, and he was eating Chinese food with his friends in bed. I couldn't understand why he would come here to eat. Today, I looked in; he was knocked out asleep, with a puffy face and abrasions over his eyes. I had to look twice to make sure it was him. I saw the Chinese containers, he didn't look better; it's unbelievable, or am I? I mean, like, where are we valley girl?*

*I sat down to write about yesterday, today, and now.*

*In the afternoon yesterday, I went to the AIDS Resource Center, and I met Bill Hunt. Bill runs the Resource Center. Bill makes life easier and more bearable for people from whom others want to run from. He provides food and feeds people whom others would not even eat in the same room with. Bill Hunt offers unconditional love and support for people. He opens his heart and arms and embraces people others do not want to touch. And all his people are dying. Bill Hunt has AIDS, and he is also slowly dying. Every day they are alive, they are dying. How would that be for you? For someone you really, really love, all your love is in that person, how would that be to see them slowly die? Bill told me last week everyone around him thought that he was going to die every day. Every day last week was his last day. He couldn't get out of bed, he couldn't walk, he couldn't eat, he couldn't talk, he couldn't do anything. Every day you are alive, you are going to die. Every night you fall asleep, you don't wake again. Death is in the room for you all the time, grabbing your arm, trying to rip you from all that you know. But you know what happen with Bill? Alongside death, every day, every night, every minute, Bill had family, friends, and strangers who brought with them love. They each brought their love for Bill. Bill was surrounded by pure love, and every minute, love fought against death, pushing back against death. And at the end of the week, death released its grip, defeated by love, and the room was filled with life. And Bill is back with life and love, giving all of it to dying people. All his life and all his love he gives. He's amazing. It doesn't matter who you are, where you are from, what you believe, or what you look like. Bill will offer you everything he has, including his life. If only there were millions of bills to balance the millions who aren't.*

*He told me all about what the* Resource Center *can do.* There are support groups for men and women with AIDS *and support groups for the family. There are services to take care of pets, people to walk your pet if you can't, housekeeping, and people who will come to do your shopping. A food pantry will give you $50 weekly of food and toiletries. All the resources available in Dallas for people with AIDS come* *together at Bill Hunt's office and he gives it all away. The Resource Center is for people diagnosed with AIDS. You have to have AIDS.*

# Chapter 9

*Friday, January 17th, 1992*


*Dear Jenny,*

*In the movie 'Hook,' Tink alludes to a place between wakefulness and sleep. It is a place where you can see and feel everything wrong with you or around you, but here you are safe, and the things that are after you can't get you in this place. Betty was just there, in that safe place while she was talking about AIDS. She knows that she is sick and that this is what will end her life, and she knows that this part is not going to change. She seems to accept death, but she is having a harder time accepting dying. With a lot of energy and willpower she tries hard to keep AIDS far from herself. She knows she will die, and that is easier for her than how she will die. She's so scared about dying, how she will feel, the pain she will feel, how she will look, her body decimated, ravaged from AIDS. She's scared she will be alone; people will have to make themselves visit her, force themselves to kiss her or hug her, this is what she doesn't want to live with or die from. She started to cry and couldn't go on. Then she recalled the first night I came into her room, and there was a glow. And then she stopped, closed her eyes, and it was over.*

*Now I'm sitting here in the dark; her eyes are closed, and she won't come back tonight. Searching for that safe place. She sees things and feels things that I seem to be blocked from.*

# **Chapter 10**



*Sunday, January 19th, 1992*


*Dear Jean,*

*Today is Sunday, and we're at the hospital to bring Betty home. The doctor informed us during Betty's discharge that she is leaving with the same infection that was responsible for 70% of her health issues ten days ago. She has an infected ulcer in her esophagus. Betty has CMV, a virus. And there is a clot in her upper right arm. Her diet remains limited but gradually improves, and her strength remains relatively low. Additionally, Betty has three valves protruding from her chest below the shoulder. She will require an IV from 8:00 p.m. to 9:00 a.m., receiving three medications through it. These medications include an antibiotic to combat the infection and Clyecleoliobunnotrentic to address the CMV, and she will also receive a Big Bump.*

*The Big Bump is a super-powered mix of nutrients, calories, proteins, neutrons, electrons, and protons. It keeps Betty healthy since she can't eat, it's a substitute for food. This is how things are. We're here to support her. Living with someone who's nearing the end of their life, what will that be like? There's gotta be a way forward. There's always a way because we always end up somewhere. We always reach a point in time, so there's gotta be a way that we got there. Where's that destination? What's it like? How will we get there? As we pick our path, look at the things that might get in our way. If it was easy, we could say, "Our journey will be filled with love." "I'll keep reminding myself to see, bring, and feel love."*

*Then with love by your side and everyone around you armed with love we are stronger, we can't lose. We've learned over the years, over countless centuries of history, that when love leads the way you get there.*

*It's not easy.*

# **Chapter 11**

*Hello Jenny,*

*It seems like it is so much later, it's 7:30 p.m. The past 8 hours have been dripping thick with sadness and fear. It seems so dark. The darkness is impregnable, and you can't see anything in front of you. It has been crazy hard for Betty to be at home. She feels she should be able to do what she's always done, and can't since she is home. She can't be how she was in real life. She can't find a way to be anything that defined her before; she's scared of leaving herself behind. She has a hard time being around people because she was the one who brought comfort and joy, and right now, she can't find any comfort and no joy. She can't even begin to bring what she could before for everyone. She can't get around what is blocking her, she can't get away from what is after her, and she wants to run or move from room to room to anywhere, but it doesn't matter where she is, it's everywhere. She became so tired and scared that she began to cry, and there wasn't enough comfort in the world to be there for her. She cried because she couldn't do anything for herself; someone had to help her do everything. She cried because she could not do what people wanted her to do. She cried about how physically bad and painful she felt. She cried because how will anyone want to be around her? How will anyone care for her? NO ONE, WILL WANT TO! It was so unreal, unworldly, it seemed beyond life. The thoughts and feelings were not from her living, they were thoughts of her dying.*

*Betty is still accepting parts of having AIDS. Sometines she hardly thinks that it has anything to do with why she was in the hospital. She still wants to work four days a week so that she won't crumble away. She doesn't want to stop anything, if she stops, then it must be the end. You can't escape from what is in front of you. It's not going away. Neither will we. We have to live with what is right there. Betty, being at home is going to be beyond what we know. It is going to be everywhere.*

*I don't know. What else is going on that matters? Denver seems so far away, as if I'm living another life. What do you think this will do for our marriage? Sometimes people are drawn closer together when they come close to the edge. Other times it slowly fades away and the marriage ends. I'm unsure where we are. There still has to be enough love and caring left to continue. I don't know. Things are hard, like money, a job, or change, maybe. It starts to get comfortable alone.*

*I started exercising last Saturday morning. I'm trying to do so every other day. We will see; it is probably my 100th attempt at exercising. My room here is nice, clean and quiet. I hung up Ryan's collage that she made and Tessa's snowflake. It's a nice room to hang out in. I try to think about the 'egg' in our relationship.*

*I borrowed some of the Nature of the Soul thought and thought that a place to start is to describe the 'egg.' It's hard to explain. Different circumstances seem to block our relationship. It could be how one of us does something or we say something, and it's wrong, but if it is seemingly wrong, then some intent is there, so each is responsible. I can't say, "I didn't mean it like that," because somewhere I did. If that's what it became, then it had to be that, life doesn't spring from nothing. Before it became that, it was that. So then after "I didn't mean anything," it creates more stuff and slowly we become that stuff and our relationship becomes that. Before you know it, you could have some pretty wild stuff.*

*You can create whatever you want, well, almost anything, but maybe you can. If you take what you want and peel it back, it will reveal the emotion. "I want a trip to Disneyland," peel it back, maybe a few layers and you will reveal happiness, fun. Well, I can create that; I can do it right now, although granted, it may not be as fun as the Matterhorn, dumb example. We can create what we want in our relationship, I don't know. You have a relationship and marriage that begins with love, trust, caring and support, good things, so then it seems like what ever else comes along, it can be dealt with by those four things, but it doesn't always. It looks like more was made up in the beginning than it was.*

# Chapter 12

*Monday, January 20th, 1992*

*Dear Jean,*

*I'm at Eckert's filling a prescription. I didn't get too much done today. I was able to work out for a while, so maybe I have that going for me. It has been a rather hectic day, and I can feel it all over my body. Betty got out of bed and we helped her move down the hallway to the den. She can sit on the couch for a short while and quickly becomes uncomfortable, then we help her back down the hallway to her bedroom where she tries to sleep and escape the pain. The discomfort and pain she has is physical and is quickly followed by emotional pain when she looks around and sees and feels where everything is going. She has trouble sleeping at night and stays in bed tossing and turning. I listen to the sounds of the night through a monitor and I sleep the same way. I can hear her fears and her cries during the night.*

*Earlier in the day while Betty was resting, I went to*

*Ally's to play basketball with Nick, Ben, and Corey. How do you think I did? I still had a game.*

*During the game Betty called and was getting restless. She wanted someone to come to her house and be with her. So I'm on my way home after a stop at Eckert's. It is like the calm before an anticipated storm with Betty. I get nervous when Betty is restless. She gets mad. She doesn't know what to do or what will happen, but she knows there is an end and she's scared and restless. Who wants to die? Right now things are huge to her, and she lashes out, often, at everything, trying to stop whatever is after her. She doesn't know what it is or where it may strike and she tries to keep it away daily. It is going to hurt so much. They just called my name, my prescription is ready, see you later.*

*Later. I talked to Dr. Pounders, trying to find out something and hear something about why Betty is so sick. What are the meds? What are the three IVs doing? Where are we at? Has anything changed? Please change. I don't know anything. Pounders says that the CMV, an AIDS virus that Betty has, was diagnosed in December. The CMV is in an ulcer and on her esophagus. There is no medication to change anything. On average, it takes 6 to 9 to 12 months. There are exceptions. The fact that her body organs are okay indicates no correlation to anything. Nothing that happens physically indicates anything. Getting worse doesn't mean it won't get better, and getting better doesn't mean it won't get worse. They can tell you how everything is in the body but can't tell you how it may be the next day or week. With AIDS things may happen in stages. There is no telling how long each stage will last; it may be just a week, and then something else starts to happen, and that may last a day, a month, or six months. The variation is pretty wide for each patient, and Betty is female. Betty is always the only female patient in her doctors and clinic's waiting rooms. People see a mother bringing her son for appointments or treatments. Nobody sees a son bringing a mother. They look at me, not her.*

*Many questions and answers either don't exist or seem elusive.*

*Betty has heard her prognosis under lighter circumstances; she ignores it or doesn't want to listen. She has her plan, and she has her prognosis about how long she is going to live and probably how she is going to die. She sometimes acts or thinks she is not sick, which is weird. She knows very little about AIDS, none of us know much. So we need to do something, something that will somehow help Betty put her heart to rest. She just woke up. I can hear her gagging and crying for Big Mike, who is asleep. Betty has a massive fear of choking in her sleep. She is afraid that one morning she won't wake up. It is sad. I don't know what will happen or where it will go. From here it all looks so big. I'm going to go, she's crying, love to you and the girls, now and forever.*

*I love the egg!*

# Chapter 13



*Jenny,*

*It is so hard to tell sometimes. You know, it is like you are just out there, wandering. You don't know where you are, where you are going or what is going on. You don't even always know why you might be going anywhere.*

*Betty is mixing dreams with reality and all of her time with the present. She goes back and forth, the present to the past, reality to dreams. It's all mixed up in her head and then she gets scared because she doesn't know where or when she is. She gets so confused, she can't tell the difference because everything is so fucking real to her. She's living over her whole life, parts of her past are her present again. And it is all so real. What if it's like the reported 'white light passing in front of you, only slowly. She wants to know if we painted faces and hair on the wooden dolls. She wants to know if her mother is here. She's been crying most of the evening because she is convinced that there are people in gray coats who are coming to take her. And she cries out, fear hastening her speech, "Wayne, Wayne, who are those people in the gray coats that keep coming for me? Don't leave me." and she cries and cries, you can't comfort her. I sit on her bed, running my fingers through her hair, trying to soothe her. I am petrified, can't move by what is happening.*

*Jeff just called.*

*It is later, and I'm trying to take it easy, my mind goes back to the prognosis. Betty was crying earlier today, saying that in one year, she will be worse than she is now and then in 2 years, she will even be worse. She thinks she will be sick and live for 2 years, which would make it January 1994. I'm not sure 6-month prognosis means 2 years. I don't know what to think, Betty seems weak and every time she gets sick and then well again, she stays a little weaker or a little sicker. How long can someone's body maintain like this? How long can one's body keep taking the drugs that she is taking? Jeff seems to think it's out there towards 2 years also. I asked Tracy about it, and she changes the subject. Tracy won't go near the end. Maybe Jeff and Betty are right, I don't know, I'll leave it alone.*

*You know something, of all of us it's Tracy. Betty and Tracy and how fortunate they are. Part of it is they are the same person, they're not twins, that's 2 people, they're 1 people, there is so much of Betty in Tracy. What they think, what they like to do, how they look, sit, talk, everything. They're each other somehow. And they care for each maybe a bit beyond where I've been.*

# Chapter 14

*Hello,*

*Well, it's been raining most of the afternoon, my legs are sore from exercising and from whatever else I did today;*

- *I went to Richland College for Continuing Education class schedule to see if Betty may be interested in doing something.*

- *I went to the library and checked out some old movie books for Betty to look at; she likes that old stuff, the glamor.*

- *Picked up the backyard that was full of these little itty bitty dog droppings.*

- *Put Betty's bathroom back together after painting it.*

- *Made an appointment with the AIDS Resource Center to go back and learn about Social Security, Disability, and workman's compensation.*

- *Change plans for the fifth time on how to deal with Betty's work.*
- *Called Sharon Chambers about my money because I'm broke and my transcript had to be revised and sent back for final approval before I'm certified.*
- *Made dinner and brownies.*

*Bad news Jean, love of my life, this transcript stuff may delay me working when I get back to Denver, my teaching certificate is being held up for my final transcripts. I am very sorry, I will be working soon. Seems unreal, wife, two kids and no job. I guess, fortunately right before having to quit banking and start teaching, I was laid off from banking. Personal lending is being phased out, no personal decisions, a mathematical loan equation will spit out whether you are worthy or not. So we do get unemployment and qualify for retraining money from Denver County, so it's a bit. There's a way.*

# **Chapter 15**

*Dear Jenny,*

*What a day. I don't think I've ever had a day like this. When you called, I was a bit overwhelmed. I had just walked to the back porch, I was trying to breathe. I was hyperventilating, I couldn't breathe, my breath had been taken away, and I was about to follow. Betty was talking about her sadness and her pain. It seems Betty slowly deals with what she can handle. Like it is so big, chunks at a time. She was trying to deal with a little more of it and when she does it's so painful for her, you can't help but lose yourself in her pain. She was trying to deal with work and the fact that it has to end.*

*Betty was in her 40s when she went back to school to be a nurse. and she loved it from the first class to her graduation. She was so excited and it was a huge triumph for her. She did it. She was married at 18, and quickly had six kids. And when she was done raising kids and her marriage was ending, she went back to school and became a nurse. For her, it was like, here I am, married, kids, divorced and now I am at my most powerful, my most beautiful. It was everything for her. That's how it was and now all of that has to be left behind. She has only worked a couple of times since Thanksgiving and has been on extended leave. It is hard for her to let go of work and she's so scared about her work finding out what is wrong with her, scared and saddened by what people will think of her. You know what people think about people with AIDS. I doubt there has ever been such a scorn upon disease. What do you think people with AIDS see when people see them. She is afraid that if she quits, she will wilt away and die. And all of these things and all these horrors are twisting and turning inside of a beautiful mother.*

*I went to Presbyterian Hospital today. I had a small list of what we wanted, it was peanuts but we thought it would really help out. First Big Mike and I met with Chris Grossner, manager of Presbyterian benefits. Chris seemed like a nice enough guy, but while we were talking it seemed a lot of issues and ideas were flying right by, he was only able to see a small square role, he knew nothing or could do nothing but beyond his cardboard box size job. I left that meeting concerned about Chris's ability or desire to handle our small request. Big Mike went home, and I started walking around the hospital, looking for payroll to pick up Betty's check and thinking of what to do next. When I was done thinking, I was standing directly across from the Administration and the office of Bill Haire, CEO and Chairman of Presbyterian. So I went in, and I asked to see the CEO. To my amazement, his secretary, after asking my name and why I was here, took me into the CEO's office. I was impressed, but then not really prepared. I told the CEO about Betty being a nurse here at Presbyterian and about Betty having AIDS and not really wanting to quit her job. I told him what we had requested from Chris Grossner, mentioned the box Chris is stuck in, and the CEO promised that he would call Chris and see to it that our requests would be 'considered and handled.' I felt a little better that maybe there would be some sort of consideration, geez, I know that I would do that. Also though, considered and handled are not the most positive response, we will see. Same deal here, there's always a way to do whatever you are doing.*

*I ran 1.5 miles today and felt pretty good, yippee.*

*Tracy came by, and she became very worried about Betty. Something is going on with Betty, she is so sad and down about everything, and she's so sad and upset about her work. It's so unreal here, and stuff is always happening. It is not like working at a bank.*

# Chapter 16

*Thursday, January 23rd 1992*

*My Dearest Jenny,*

*It was fun and good to talk to everyone tonight. Ryan is a good kid, as she is beginning to get older, you can hear confidence and interest when she talks. She has a wide range of thoughts that go beyond things that are just there. She's still great. There are times when she seems to be busting at the seams. The confidence is still there. The interest and thoughts, at times get a bit wild.*

*Tessa sounded like she was getting better. It was too bad that she was so sick. Christmas came and went by so quickly that it was already a month later. I missed the time after Christmas when the kids were playing with their presents. There's a window of opportunity there to play and find something new with the kids. It comes, and then it goes. You sounded well. I hope it is not too bad in Denver without me. Maybe not, you would have to think so, I guess, maybe not, isn't it? It's like that song where the distressed girl is almost crying, "Is she as pretty as me, huh?" I miss you. I feel a little refreshed about what I must do in Denver. Refreshed in that side of my life, parts of my life feel good. And yet, I cut you off tonight on the phone. Very sorry. I did want to hear what you had to say, but I didn't know what you were saying. I guess, no 'buts', I'm how I am, imperfect is a world judged for perfection. It must be hard. I don't know, we could go anywhere with our marriage. I love you, Jenny. I hope all is well with you, and I look forward to seeing you.*

*Hey, it is a little later in the night. All is well, Betty did pretty well today. She was awake most of the day. She took a bath and was out on the couch for a while. It was good to see her alive and out of her room. The couch is big, it is actually one great big quadruple seater couch, one great big double seater couch, and one great big single seater. It's big enough to swallow the little kids. I've seen Spike and Emma crawl out from the mouth of the couch.*

*It feels good that Betty is up and out a little bit. It is so hard to tell how she will be. She improves from bed to bath to the couch, maybe to the car, and she seems to plow ahead, not seeing or not wanting there to be any limits to what she is doing. That's part of the deal here, we don't know what is moving Betty to do what she may do. We are not in her head that may be filled with terrifying thoughts and images. We aren't in her heart that is full of fear and sadness. It's like, let's say Betty gets up and starts to sweep the kitchen, and we say, "Betty, don't do that, we can do it for you." What we say or how we respond comes from our heads, which will not comprehend or understand what is in her head or her heart. If we don't try to understand that then we miss what is happening beyond her sweeping the kitchen. She's dealing with the loss of herself and maybe sweeping is how she tries to hold on to something. You gotta have something.*

*Tomorrow I go back to Presbyterian at 11:00 a.m. to see what Chris Grossner has done. He called today and said that the Big Cheese had called him. Chris said that he will review everything with the Big Cheese, big deal. I hope it goes better than some of the things since being in Big D. It's getting late, 10:45 p.m. a new day tomorrow. The days fly by, 10 minutes are gone in a minute, and every time I turn around, it's 45 minutes later.*

*Ah, listen. You hear that, it's Betty, she starting to cry. I can't hear what she is saying, only the cries. It's not a loud sobbing cry, it's a soft cry that you hear beyond the darkness. Big Mike is with her now. I can hear the whispers, still no words. I lie here in my own darkness. Betty cries. Sometimes it flows from her, and it seems as total as sadness can be, it flows out, it gets out of her. The sadness and fear that tears at her fills her with tears and she cries. The tears bring tears.*

*Sweet dreams, Jenny, give the girls a kiss and a hug. Thanks for the prayers and the meditation. I remembered the class last night while I was lying around, and I made a connection with the class. I spent most of the time with you.*

*Love, Wayne*

# Chapter 17

*Friday, January 24th, 1992*

*Dear Jenny,*

*The deal keeps coming back to finding a way to do something. It sort of seems that during an unordinary day in our lives, you would expect yourself to be able to draw upon the strength, energy, and desire of something to be able to do more than you do in your ordinary life, and as I sit here quietly, with deep breaths I can feel the strength, energy, and desire just barely trickle into my body.*

*I miss you and the kids.*

# Chapter 18

*Saturday morning, January 25th, 1992*

*Good morning Jenny,*

*What is it like for you this morning? I am having a seat in Big Mike and Betty's backyard. It is so nice, like a bit of heaven. I wonder if you find a place or go to a place that is beautiful, if you need to be anywhere else. This looks as beautiful as a king's garden, so it can be right there for you, you have to give it life.*

*Yesterday I almost fell asleep out here, it is really something else. There are green bushes that circle the yard, a tall tree in the corner that still has brown leaves, a nice long stone walk that takes you around the yard, there are stones that border beds, and over underneath the tall tree, there is a deer. It's not real dear. I've heard at least six different birds chirping and singing. If I was a bird I'd sing all the time.*

*The weather has been nice since Betty came home from the hospital, and since I really don't have much to do, I'm resting in the backyard and taking it easy. Yesterday, I met with Chris Grosner, he hadn't met with the big cheese yet, so I wondered why he met with me. I have had moments of doubt recently about how I will handle some of this stuff.*

*I worry that if the hospital does nothing and if there is no consideration of Betty working at the hospital, it would be hard. Betty thinks that she has been good to the hospital and a good employee. Sort of the image of an old-fashioned employee who gave the company all that she had. She knows that we are talking to the hospital, but she doesn't know exactly what we are doing or asking for. I think she would like some sort of acknowledgment or recognition for what she has done in her life. The hospital has a chance to do that, and if they don't, we will look for other ways. I hope that the hospital will do something. It is hard sometimes to impress upon people. They have their own deal and their own agenda. I remain optimistic, with some lingering caution about the outcome with the hospital.*

*Today, Betty has remained in bed, she has a sharp pain in her side that makes her very uncomfortable. She says the pain is not constant, but she can feel the pain coming back each time, and as it gets closer and closer and stronger and stronger, she feels it, fears it until it grips her insides and squeezes down hard till it hurts, stays hurt and then it slowly goes away, recedes till called upon again to deliver pain and she waits until the next time.*

*Yesterday she had a bath, got dressed, and Tina came over. It was a very tearful hello, and they were both rather shocked and scared for each other. There was a short acknowledgment of AIDS, and when AIDS was mentioned again, it was always in the third person, AIDS outside of Betty. Trying to push it away. Tina is a wonderful great friend of Betty's. Like blood sisters. They went to school together, they graduated together and then they went to work together at Presbyterian. They were both very much alike. They both looked alike, both beautiful, knowing it, they were a pair at the hospital. You may have heard of Betty and Tina. And they thought alike, they were sisters from different parents.*

*Betty had been pretty anxious about talking to Tina, it was another acknowledgment that she was sick. It seemed to go well, and they sat in Betty's room for a couple of hours, confirming their friendship and their care for one another.*

*Friday night, I went to Tracy's. So did Diddy and her six-person entourage, also Mark and Katie, Blake, Tommy, Max and Ally, Corey, Zach, Lauren as well as Tracy's family, Nick, Ben, Daniel, Spike and Emma and a new kid. There sure are a lot of kids for a couple of kids. It was lots of fun. It was quickly midnight, I disappeared and drove home.*

*Well, it is time for lunch, and Betty said that she wanted to get up. Guess what is for lunch? My favorite lunch; hot dogs, chips and dip, and I have a TV for sports.*

*See you, take care, Wayne.*

*Linda called, Aunt Barbara's dying. My heart soars for Aunt Barbara and everything that she did for us when Betty was dying. Betty asked Barbara to help us, and Barbara did. Barbara had angel dust in her.*

# Chapter 19

*Super Bowl Sunday, January 26th, 1992*

*Dear Jenny,*

*It is 3:00 p.m., and I am under the covers, sick, real sick; my stomach is a painful tight knot, being pulled around my insides; I can feel it everywhere. I haven't been able to eat, not even my favorite lunch, and I couldn't watch the Super Bowl preview. I tried to drink some ginger ale, but it was too cold. Tracy and all of her kids were vomiting last night from both ends. Ally called, and she just got sick and is in bed for the rest of the day. Add to this a very cold, wet day, and you will end up with nothing. I have been sick and chilled all Super Bowl Sunday Day. Oh well, I think of the Super Bowl I went to with Wild Billy and his friend Vaughn in Miami. Cowboys. That was an incredible Super Bowl weekend. We did things I didn't get to do and rarely if ever since. Rats.*

*Oh no, my stomach. I've just made it back to bed after*

*watching the end of the Super Bowl. I'm glad that I didn't bet, the Bills lost. I would have lost everything: the house, the kids, my wife, everything. I am a terrible better. Thanks for the picture; it was nice to see the kids. It is wild that I am where I am. I will be back, and we will go from there to somewhere else.*

*It begins a new week. Betty is feeling pretty well, we'll try to get out of the house for a while, if we don't, things are fine.*

*I don't know if I had told you, but I revised my certification book, and I mailed it back on Friday, but, and it is a really pretty big butt; I will still have to send the final draft out after this, hopefully soon, you are a saint.*

*Take care, Jenny, I will see you soon, love.*

# Chapter 20



*Tuesday, January 28th 1992*


*Hey Jean,*

*I just spoke with you for the fourth time today, it's been great. Jeff is in town to fight a speeding ticket. They didn't dismiss it as he was hoping, so he will be back in 2 weeks to continue his small conquest, a conquest nonetheless and that's probably needed in our lives. We win.*

*There are times when Betty has a lot of anger, or madness that comes from the fear. She wants something to make a difference and it doesn't. She wants to get back at people for something, anybody for anything, and she can't, I don't know. In the course of the day there are things that are dealt with confrontationally. It is like she wants to get somebody back for what is happening to her. "I am going to get you." It is like walking on eggshells and Betty will say anything, it flies out everywhere bouncing off walls till it hits someone. Never one of her kids. Then the attack becomes focused, a direct hit and Bam, it hurts. Anger, madness and fear is what is around us. Sometimes it's like you want to yell "it doesn't matter!" But back again, who are you to say what matters to someone, you don't know, you can't decide what matters to someone who is dying. There's a kid and she told me once, "while you were telling me I need to go to school, I was thinking of how to kill myself." And it was like "oh no, my god help me, I fucked up." I'm not even on the same planet with what matters to this kid. You don't know.*

*Betty also has an image that she promoted for co-workers, Harry, and Big Mike. An image that she is tough enough, strong enough, mean enough to make it just like others, and in doing so, she became so. I always thought a philosopher said "You become who you continually are" and we hardly notice while we become how or who we are. She's done well and where she ended up is not that bad. She did a lot of stuff, enjoyed many many days, lived in a big comfortable house, everything was good, and then AIDS, it will end with AIDS. It's a complicated picture, tough as she is, maybe she got it from all the shopping that she did with Tracy and Ally. But how she is, wasn't always like she was. There's a bigger side of Betty where she was wonderfully thoughtful of others. She had a heart full of fondness and tenderness for many people especially for kids. She used to bring me Slim Jims, Heath bars and Good and Plenty, she always knew what I liked and what I needed, every time she knew and every time she was right there. If anything ever happened to one of her kids, she could not go on. I don't imagine how people manage with such tremendous pain and loss. Betty raised six kids, Linda, Laurie, Jeff, myself, Ally and Tracy. It was during the '60s and '70s. It was a big family and we were all over the place, there was so much to do, the world around us awakening and we did our own share. I don't know, just seems so hard, she's having a crash course on dying, the loss of your life and leaving behind all of your work and life.*

*This week is coming to a screeching halt. Tomorrow I'm going to write a letter to a private high school in Denver and ask them to send me an application. How is everyone in Denver? Our neighbors, how are they doing? What is your mom up to? How is she? Tell everyone I say hi. Good night Jenny, I wish you were in my arms, holding each other, feeling you next to me. You know what is wild, the times that you want to run from everything is the same time that you want to be held.*

*Love, Wayne*

# Chapter 21

*Wednesday, January 29th, 1992*

*Dear Jenny,*

*Lying before me are forms and bills of all kinds: insurance forms, AIDS Resource Center forms, medical bills, gas bills, car bills, insurance bills, water bills, credit card bills, ducks with bills, consent forms, and a Will. And I look at all these forms and bills, and it's like, golly, where do you start? You start with a list. So I made a list and am working on it. If everyone that I talk to on the phone would each do just a little bit, if everyone everywhere would do just a little bit, then it would work out, but too many people are off the wall. I am void of thinking of being involved in the implications of all these forms, bills, and wills.*

*Betty is too sick to get out of bed today. She's so sick, feels so bad, she can't eat anything, she can't sleep, and she tosses and cries out from the torment of being sick and the idea of dying. I can't imagine knowing I was dying, even if it's not for months or a year. Death is there, and it's there where nothing else will be. No more people, no more things, no more kids, death is the no more of anything. I guess at the exact moment you die, you don't know what happened, you don't know anything, you're dead, everything stops. All that is left is your spirit, it becomes alive in each person that you touched. Each person you are alive with has your spirit and it lives on in their life. It's hard right now for Betty. It's like one of those things you think about how you will be, but then you get there. When you're not there, it's like, "Yeah, when my time comes, I'll be ready," you fuckin think? Then, when you're there, when death is there, you don't recognize anything. It's like we have no idea how we will be when we get to certain things. It seems our minds are not capable of understanding death without the experience. Your being changes. I don't know, Betty will, she's the one there. I can't do much. I sit and listen and try to go away inside of myself. When you were a kid or an adult, when you're alive, was there ever a place you would go to and try to beat it into your head that this is not really happening to me. It makes my heart pound, and I can hardly breathe.*

*Sometimes, it is everywhere: the sights, the smells, the sounds, and the feelings. All of the senses are acute to the magnificence and the hugeness of being sick. Goodbye, I am going there now.*

*Hey Jean, It's later, after afternoon, Wednesday. It's been Wednesday forever. How is the group going? I remember being in a group talking about what I was afraid of. What am I afraid of? There are things real and unreal that I'm afraid of. And it's hard to sit and recognize or verbalize what it is that you're afraid of, so I'm not going to do that, but I will try to connect with the group and try to connect to anything.*

*I was with Betty this morning, in and out of her being.*

*In the afternoon, I met with John Gaddis. John is the intake person at the AIDS Resource Center. I missed my first appointment with John last week because I thought the appointment was at 3:00, and it was at 1:00. Today's appointment was at 3:00, and I was here at 1:00. Something is upside down here, and I'm tumbling. There were things that happened and things that were said, and somehow John and I were different, more than that, we seemed not to like each other. I was sitting in my seat, squirming in my chair, thinking that there was no way that this meeting was going to be worth it or work out. I started crawling down underneath the table like in the Hagger commercial. It was a mess. John is a strong, firm-looking man of about 35 years of age. He wore tight black pants, black high tops, a black jacket, and a gold t-shirt. This sounds stupid, but he looked like a male model, Mr January. But slowly the light came out of the darkness. It took three long hours until we slowly came around to a respectful relationship. And I am so wrong judging people. All the judgments that I make about people get in the way and set up blocks. I don't know. I'm not always a good person. You know how many flaws I have?*

*John knew a lot about HIV and AIDS. John's brother, his lover, his friends, and his therapist are all HIV+, and he too felt like me, that he was upside down, tumbling around, smashing against things. He has been a social worker since July 1991 and he wants to move and get away from AIDS. He wants to escape the pain and sadness and dying, which is like bolts of lightning striking so many in his life. John talked about how the deaths around him have been plagued by the horrible stigma of the disease. AIDS has brought a lot of attention to the gay community, and it hasn't been pleasant; he and his friends feel disgusted by other people; imagine that, you can't, there is no way I could imagine what it must be like, and while dying and in death, he said it gets worse. He's heard people say, "oh, he is better off dead". That is so wrong. Fuck you. Fuck me. I'm an ass. There's a lot of caring in the gay community because there are so many who don't care. Caring. That is what John is doing. He was caring for me. He cares and I'm an ass. It was a good meeting. John was very helpful and focused on my questions about AIDS. The questions have no answers that are the same for anyone. There is a big variance in people who are HIV+. You know what gets crazy? There are some things I don't want to know about that may happen next, but then you want to know if she's going to get better, you don't want to know if she's going to get worse. Do you want to know if she's going to hurt and suffer? Will she cry? Every night? There are no answers. There are different viruses that affect each person differently. There's never a time to say definitely when anything may happen, all these different things may happen, even all at once, and they may not. You don't know, it's upside down and back and forth or it doesn't come back at all, it's hard to know what is coming and going.*

*They do know stuff about CMV. CMV is an AIDS virus Betty has. It is usually in the eyes. It attacks the eyes and eats away at the sun. People first become blurry, then objects lose their shapes and sizes and then all you can see is their heart, then everything disappears. But it is not going to eat away at Betty's eyes. It's going to eat her esophagus. Betty has CMV on or in her esophagus. The CMV is going to eat her esophagus and then if she is alive her stomach will be eaten. From the inside out. The treatment, Cytovene, is to try and slow down the CMV from destroying and spreading. Cytovene is effective anywhere from 6 to 24 months at which time the CMV becomes stronger and immune to the Cytovene, and then it spreads through the body and nothing can stop it. It hides in other cells, it takes on characteristics of other cells and it can't be found and it can't be destroyed, you are. CMV is a fairly quick killer, there is a variance and it is hard to plan for anything, you have to plan for everything. The meeting with John Gaddis was very good. Right away* *the center will pay Betty's monthly insurance premium up to $200 a month that Betty is responsible for. The money comes from the Ryan White Memorial Fund. Ryan White was young, he had hemophilia and needed a blood transfusion. He contracted HIV from the blood. He was a 14, 15 year old boy and was not accepted. People didn't want to be near him, his school didn't allow him to come to school. He and his family had to move. You know anyone that is not allowed to come to school? There is so much fear and ugliness hurled at people with HIV. He died young. Doesn't matter what you can do, there is no way you could begin to even scratch the surface of how people with AIDS feel, live and die.*

*John also authorized $50 each week that Betty can spend at a food pantry. The food pantry is in the back alley of an old building. It is much smaller than a 7-Eleven and has more food than a king Soooopers, and a heart the size of the world. The volunteers in the food pantry are very kind, helpful, talkative, and there is something else about them. Their kindness, their helpfulness, conversations didn't come from their job description or their training. It came from somewhere* *else and that's what you want to embody.*

*Right when I walked in I was greeted and introduced to the coordinator. They were kind and loaded me up with food and toiletries. The pantry serves a lot of people who have AIDS. It is a place to come for food and comfort for people from people. John gave me a list of support groups, people that will help with Social Security, people that will give haircuts, massages, run errands and take care of pets. Providing real basic necessities for people who no longer have access to the bare necessities of life.*

*I also talked to Presbyterian hospital and their answer was a crushing 'no' for our request. I don't feel like we asked for very much, for the hospital to pay her $250 monthly health insurance premium, pay the $3,000 yearly out of pocket, and to retroactive her disability payments back to November. That was all. Why did the big cheese say no, he could have justified anything with kindness. Golly. You know why they said no or at least the reason they made up they said no, was because Betty had saved enough of her own money and they decided that this amount was enough. Fuck them. I haven't said anything to anyone about* *blowing this deal with the hospital. I wonder if I should have waited or done something different. I wonder if I could have gotten Harry more involved.*

*You have to eat a lot of bullshit to survive.*

*Who knows? It is over and time to find another way. Figure out what we can do with what we have. I need to see what she owes, see about paying it off and put together some sort of budget. All these budgets I do I should have been a banker. Not everything works out. But it can't get in our way or stop us from doing what we need to do or what we want to do. I have to remember there are always more ways to do the same thing, just have to find that way or is it the other way. Well good night Jenny, I will know tomorrow when I will see you again.*

*Love, Wayne*

# Chapter 22

*Thursday, January 30th, 1992*

*Dear gems of all gems,*

*The sun is out strong today, finally, after so many days of dreary weather, the sun is shining triumphantly and we can go outdoors. It's mid-afternoon. I just finished my favorite lunch, and I'm now resting in the backyard. The drag about this is that this is my last piece of paper, so this must be goodbye; if I can no longer write, remember that I love you very much, miss you very much, and will be with you.*

*Love, Wayne*

*PS. I called about airplane tickets home. The cheapest is an airline named Fun country or Sun Country. They fly people from the West and Midwest to fun places in the sun in the Caribbean and Mexico. The drag is that*

they only have one plane that flies everywhere, and the
next time it goes from Dallas to Denver is Wednesday,
February 12th. Now, that sounds forever and is a little
longer than I thought. Sorry about this if it is too long
since I'm gone, it is isn't it?

# Chapter 23

*Friday, January 31st, 1992*

*Dear Jenny,*

*Wondering if you could hear the birds singing. There's something that is both energizing and then draining about having so many moments in the day. The backyard is amazing. It's surrounded by a tall wooden fence; inside the fence right now, there are three birds that I cannot see, and they are calling back and forth between them. The sun is behind the tall branchy tree, casting long shadows across the yard. You can find yourself in a place that seems so beautiful, the most beautiful, and it's right in front of you.*

*Hey again. It is much later now, about 2:00 p.m. Tracy and three kids, Ally, Lauren, and Tina, came over. I'm back out in the yard resting, letting my thoughts go. We got a lot done today: I paid off a loan, taxes, and three credit cards. Since the hospital did nothing, we are trying to get most of the stuff paid off, see what is* *left, and then move on. F*** them. How do you like my banking? Debt is not good. I'd rather it be paid and done with. It's not always how much you make as much as how much you owe that screws you. Something else came up; Betty and I started talking about a place, something like the Farm. She wants a place that all the kids and grandkids could go to and visit. The Farm we had growing up, it was in upstate New York, Millerton. Long ago Harry was a nearby bystander when someone was trying to rip off the Duchess. Harry intervened and saved the Duchess. The Duchess was married to Blackjack, and their empire was in Millerton, N.Y., and Palm Beach. Blackjack died, and the Duchess married Clarence 'Porky' Manero. St. Clarence is my confirmation name. Since Harry helped the Duchess, years later the Duchess helped Harry build the Farm on her farm property, Tummy Acres, in Millerton, N.Y., and that is where we would go for holidays and for the summer. Betty wants a place like that, a place where people could go to visit, a place maybe where we would keep some of Betty's things together. Some of the ideas began as we were walking through the house recently. When we passed the fireplace, Betty asked me if I wanted the picture*

83

*always cared and always looked out for me. "mother, did it have to be so hard." Pink Floyd, The Wall.*

*And I saw her do that with each of her kids. Her love for us could not be stopped by the things that we did; she was amazing. Whatever we did, she always loved us . And there were so many new and exciting things going on in the '60s and '70s. It was wild.*

*Well, it is even later now, it's 5:30 p.m., and I have been writing this letter all day long, and it's not finished. I managed to fill the bird feeder with bird food. The color of the bird feeder matches the fence and sits on the top of a long, thin pole.*

*Later in the afternoon, I drove with Betty to meet Harry at Black Eyed Pea. It didn't take long when Betty told him that her prognosis was 9 to 12 months, and after she said that, Betty kissed Harry. They've known each other for more than 45 years, together for almost 30 years; not sure how it ended; all the kids had moved out, and there was a big empty house. Harry may have always had girlfriends, and Betty was working with friends. One of her patients was Big Mike. And try as Harry did with a Mercedes and a new house, each of them was done with each other. It was over. And it went back a bit, and things were very comfortable at Black Eyed Pea. There was caring, there was some type of loving between them. The things that drove them apart vanished, probably not to come back between them. The empty void was filled with them together again. At this point, there were not a lot of things that mattered to them, and when nothing else mattered between them, they were talking like they had just met. Like there was no history between them that got in the way of their love. When you meet, there's hardly a history, it was like they went back to when they first met, to what brought them together. Man there is a lot of cool stuff you can do with your heart. The heart creates.*

*After her prognosis, Betty said she wanted her and Harry to help get Linda a house. Betty wanted to do this, and she wanted us all to have a house or a home to go to.*

*She somehow mentioned their love and that after all these years, she would die in love. She was very sincere. And then Betty started talking about dying and leaving everyone. Betty's not afraid of death, she's terrified of dying with AIDS. She's so afraid and saddened to leave her kids. Betty told Harry she wanted to die when all that was left was the pain. She doesn't want to live with pain. She doesn't want people to see her in pain. She doesn't want to suffer. She doesn't want people to see her suffer. And she didn't. Harry stretched way beyond himself to try and understand what Betty was saying. Harry is with God on this. Only God decides when we live and when we die. God decides how much pain we are in and how much suffering there is. How much sadness can we endure.*

*You know, it was all rather nice, sort of surreal sitting there drinking iced tea at Black Eye Pea with Betty and Harry.*

*It is now 8:00 p.m. I tell you, the hours seem like minutes. The other deal is that...*

*Betty just woke up; see you.*

# Chapter 24

*Saturday, February 1st 1992*

*Good morning Jenny,*

*It seems like Sunday, and it is Saturday. It seems like 8:00 a.m., and it is noon. It is a little overcast, no birds have come for food today.*

*I have again been wondering about Betty's prognosis. Betty talks about it often. She tries desperately to come within miles of what it all means. She wants to know, and she wants to make plans. Dr Pounders maintains that people with CMV virus will average 9 to 12 months, six months before the CMV spreads. He adds to this that people who can change their lives can live up to 2 years; you have to change your life. Changing your life I think is huge, so does Betty. She doesn't think she can change; it's so hard. I've hardly changed. Maybe you have to redefine what it means to change your life. Define it so that it fits for you. If you look out there and it's dark, and it's scary, and you've* been there before, you have to draw upon your strengths, and it is hard to do in the dark. Betty is in a dark time in her life, don't you think? And she's strong, she's stood up to everything, she's fearless, she has an endless amount of love for her kids, she's a nurse, she cares and heals people. Those are her strengths; she's strong, loving, caring, and healing, and these have to lead you through the darkness. You'll see a light, and her light is her kids and grand kids. Betty talks about being a happy child. She grew up in Queens, New York, and enjoyed living with her mother and two sisters, June and Barbara, and she liked school. New York was safe; she and her friends were young and would travel on the train to Manhattan for movies and shows, and she loved all of it. Betty was still really young, 16, and she was working at the Fannie Farmer Candy store when she met Harry. She was swept off her feet by this dashing older man, like in the picture, the War was over and Harry was an officer in the Navy. You look at the pictures, and Harry was very handsome and Betty, she was beautiful. They were married, 1949, and she was soon a mother. Sixteen years old, you work at Fannie Farmer; 17, you're married, 18, you're a mother for the rest of her life.

*For more than 45 years she was a beautiful, wonderful mother. Betty had more of a percentage of the time being happy than not. The percentage of time that her life was good, I would say, in the high 80%. That doesn't seem bad. What percent of my life, your life, are things cool? What percent of the time are things working right, where you're loved by someone, anyone? What % of the time? I would take 80% of the time; that seems high, doesn't it? She has many times of happiness under her belt, and she is relatively at ease and at some level of peace with herself and those around her. This is what the healing will be about: getting rid of the disease and becoming at ease as Betty has been. Got to go, I will talk to you later,*

*Love*

*Wayne*

# Chapter 25

*Sunday, February 2nd, 1992*

*Dear Jenny,*

*It is Sunday morning, and I must have a lot of time to write. And I've talked to you earlier. Don't you think there are other feelings and emotions behind our words? Emotions like anxiety, resentment, anger, we can only go about this far, look, I'm stretching my fingers out, not very far, and then these emotions find their way into our words, into our tone, into our relationship, it's a drag, it's crazy. We have stuff between us. It's hard to see our future. I wonder how people do it, how do you stay together? It seems that in the course of our lives, we all go through many of the same things, and there are many people who go through these things and worse things. There's violence, there's the death of a child. I can't even begin to imagine how hard these things must be, never mind, but how can some people and couples endure them? I*

*think there has to be more to begin with. Dang, keep
blowing that.*

91

# Chapter 26



*Monday, February 3rd, 1992*

*Dear Jenny,*

*This morning while I was fixing breakfast, over 100 black birds landed in almost every spot in the backyard. They landed in the two big trees and from the kitchen I could hear a very, very loud squawking. It was as if someone had turned the volume way up on a stereo. I thought of Hitchcock's movie "The Birds," and I ran through the house, closing doors and windows.*

*My day was half busy, and there were hardly any results. I talked to Mr. Harrison about some tax questions and property transfers. Still learning. My direction often seems to be financial, and if I make mistakes, it could be a mess. I wonder who deals with this stuff in other people's situations. You have to find out quickly what you're doing. I hope that by the time it matters, we know what matters.*

*I went to Dr. Pounders' office to pick up a letter that was not ready. I sat in a traffic jam on Central Expressway due to the rainy weather, a car slipped off the road. Betty was up for a while, and we were able to get out of the house slowly. We went to Michael's. Betty loves this store. She likes all the pretty things that you can put around your house, the flowers, the frames, the figures, and all the other knick-knacks. She loves the seasonal stuff and the sales that they have are really exciting. She loves the little things that kids can make for the holidays, and she seems to have a place for everything. Lots of oohs and aahs as she wanders around and wonders how pretty something would look somewhere. We walked around and around.*

*We needed to get some material, actually thread or yarn. Betty wants to make an afghan blanket but to no avail. Colors were not right.*

*'Someone told me there's a girl out there with love in her heart and flowers in her hair.' Going to California. Led Zeppelin*

*It is good to see Betty up and able to go out and expand on what she does. She walks slowly, slowly, and can make it around. We stop often, and she'll rest for a little while. After Michaels, we came home, and she slept for a while. Then she was able to get up and we went out. Big Mike, Betty, and I went to Steak and Ale. It was a great night, and even now, I can remember almost every minute clearly. They had margaritas together, and I say together because they were so happy as we sat there. They talked, loved, laughed, and held each other. The meal was great. I had a large salad, a large potato with butter, sour cream, and bacon bits, and a large prime rib, medium. It's just like before, there's no place better than where you are sometimes. As great as it can be eating steak at Delmonico's, this is great. I don't know. It's so often right there for us. The whole thing was wonderful, the meal, Big Mike, and Betty, and I think they felt the same way. How hard it must be to love someone in situations. You wonder about all of this with Betty and Big Mike. What a deal they got. How are these things doled out to two people or to anybody? How do you get what you get? How does that happen? We make choices that lead us someplace, and our choices come with possible undesirable consequences that come with the territory, and there are also consequences that may come that are unforeseen. If I decide to go out and have a beer, the possible undesirable consequences may be that the next day, I have a hangover, a very real possibility. If I'm on a walk and I get hit by a car, it's unforeseen. How did the unforeseen get into the picture? For the driver, his choices and his undesirable consequences become my unforeseen when they intersect. Others may bring the unforeseen into your reality. I don't know. I wonder how they will hang together during everything that may happen. I wonder how our relationship compares, and we worry about what we have to deal with. If I had to guess, I would say that Big Mike and Betty would stick together during everything that arises. At the end of this, they will be together. And will we be together? I tried to talk to Betty about what I perceived to be the senselessness of wasting her energy with anger toward Big Mike's kids and what he does with them. Betty is angry. But you know what, I don't know Betty's experience or her relationship with Big Mike's kids. What if something happened, and there is a reason for her anger? I need to be careful with my judgments. Not only did I not know, but even if I knew, who am I to say what made sense? I think you can get close to what sense is, but the problem is that my sense is made through my eyes. And right now, what I see and what Betty sees is very different. I'm not in the same room with what Betty sees and feels. Anger, grief, fear, and sadness seem to go together. It's like if there is grief and sadness, then maybe you should expect some anger. And maybe part of it is Betty getting mad at them or angry at them because they are a safer, easier target for Betty.*

*I don't know, who knows? Life is hard and bad sometimes. We've all seen how bad it can be. You can hear the cries at night that say how hard it is. You can see the pain and know how bad it is. And my God, bless the people with 10 times that bad. I don't know. My sense could be the senselessness. Poor Big Mike, what in the world will happen to him?*

*Later, I just made a list for tomorrow:*

- *Finalize the Will with a lawyer. Betty and Mike began Wills 3 months ago*

- *- called Dr. Pounders about the letter for disability*

- *- called about housekeeping or something,*

- *Call about handicapped parking*

-    *Get blank tapes to record something*

*There is my tomorrow, I can't wait.*

*Sweetest of all, Wayne, all day long she sits…it's a mystery to me.*

*Somewhere in Dallas, somewhere, everywhere, every night, every moment, someone is slowly trying to find their way through the darkness. Why is it like this? Why all the loneliness in the darkness? And it can be in your own house. Yourself. It could be your own daughter. She could be in the darkness, maybe so dark she may not see any other way out, and you don't even know. She may not even know anymore. And then I went in and started busting her for not doing her homework. She's not anywhere near there. She's near the edge, ready to walk over. All she sees is down, and I didn't have a f****** clue.*

# Chapter 27

*Tuesday, February 4th, 1992*

*Dear Jenny,*

*It's a little after 6:00 p.m., and I was listening to the tape that you sent. I'm going to wait until later to finish. Betty was calling out. Thanks for sending it. Right now, Betty is out in the den telling Big Mike that she wants to be buried in Colorado. Sometime today, Betty started talking about where she wanted to go to be buried. It's crazy how things come up. You do one thing, you plant one thing, and it spouts off into something else, then another thing and that thing grows, takes shape, and leads you somewhere else, and it's unsettled. There is something directing Betty, or maybe someone who has gone before, and they know what to do. We just have to follow Betty and do what she says, and it will lead to where she wants to be and what she wants. She knows how she wants things to happen. She knows the things to get behind her and into the past. She's looked forward to know what we need to do now.*

*Anyway, the burial. Betty has a distaste for a big, endless corporate cemetery on the side of a highway. Betty wants to rest in peace, not on the side of a highway. She even mentioned Mckinney and Harry's family plot there that lends toward magnificent. There's a very big, stone Irish cross memorial that was carved in Ireland. I can not tell where she was coming from. Maybe she doesn't think she has anywhere to go. Fishkill, New York, where her mother is buried, is full. So Colorado became an idea. Betty likes the idea of being close to a place or a cabin where everybody may come. Big Mike became sad and quiet, the quiet that happens when your insides are screaming. Somewhere underneath Big Mike's defense and awkwardness, he really, really loves Betty, and it breaks his heart that Betty is dying. It terrifies him when she speaks of death. May they both live out their days in peace and love. They did, in fact, pretty much once upon a time they loved one another, loved to be with each other, and they enjoyed so many of the same things together. It's like they heard each other calling one another to come out and play and live. They went places and did things together, hobbies and stuff. They would clip things out of the newspaper to go to. They would go to classes together and do projects together. They had a lot of good times together, and everything they shared and loved is coming to an end. It will be hard to remember that part about them. It seems like their deaths will overshadow their lives, mired in blackness.*

*Betty has begun to lighten up a bit. No longer is there anticipation with tremendous anxiety about when Big Mike comes home, and Betty shaking her leg waiting to attack. Big Mike walks in and twirls his hand around, and Fritz the little dog begins a loud whiny, whelping little war dance that further infuriates Betty and brings the war. What they deal with each day hammers away at them, constantly hammers away, right on their heads, and pounds at their hearts.*

*By 1:30 p.m. today, I had done nothing on my list, and then I kicked it into gear and may not stop. The Will. That was unreal. What an evolution. During the last week that the Will was being finalized, words were spoken, feelings were shared, and confirmations were made that Betty had done the right thing and made the right decisions with her Will. It is what she wanted. It is a caring will. Her decisions were to take care where she thought the most care was needed. Betty knows what she wants and why. She believes in what she's doing. We called in the final changes to the lawyer, who will be here on Saturday to sign and notarize the final copy.*

*Dr Pounders was next. I needed a letter of disability. He was really busy all day, and I went to his office and waited. It was wild how long it took, but finally, I had the letter.*

*Then I went to Presbyterian and turned in all the releases to distribute Betty's retirement funds. The distribution will be about $50,000. It seems like a lot of money that has to go a long way. $5,000 will go to savings for the funeral expenses, $25,000 for a family place, $5,000 for bills and loans, and the rest, about $15,000, will be for spending money and expenses. She will also get about $1,000 from disability and Social Security money. So somewhere in there Betty will have about $2500 bucks a month for living expenses. She needs about $750 for bills, and the rest, about $1700 a month, is spending money, $400 a week. Betty is generous with money. If she has enough for what she* *needs, the rest will be given to others, or she'll spend money on others. It's the others that she loves. And she loves to spend money and buy everyone everything. She loves to shop, "You must have this and this.. it will look so pretty there... if you don't get it now, you never will... go ahead get it.. don't worry.. just get it."*

*Housekeeping was next, and tomorrow at 3:30 p.m. John Carla will be here from AIDS Interface to offer volunteers who will come out and assist Betty. They will come out 2 to 3 times a week for a couple of hours to help around the house or run errands. Betty says she might give this a try. I don't know if she will. Betty doesn't want someone in her house; she is afraid they will have nothing to do, and she will have to give them stuff to do, or they hang out around her. She wants friends and family around her. And then she is afraid they will do what she wants to do by herself, and also about our own privacy.*

*So we will see. AIDS Interface sounds like a group that brings everything together, including all the services. I'm not sure what they do. It would be very helpful if there was someone out there who knew what to do together, who everyone is, and what everyone can do, so maybe this is the place.*

*What else was on my list?*

- *Nothing on the Buddy for Betty.*

- *Missed Ally's friend.*

- *Handicap is sending me an application.*

- *No library.*

- *No blank tape.*

- *No thread. We did get pretty close on this but were unable to find 42 oz. from the same dye lot.*

*Sometimes it's hard to get things done. She wants to knit Afghans for the place that we may get; she likes to knit, and it would be a cool thing to do. That was it for the day. Tomorrow at 10:00 a.m. Social Security calls for a telephone interview. At noon, we meet Harry for lunch, and at 3:30, we meet John Carlo from Interface.*

*And now, Betty wants to go and make funeral arrangements before she dies. We started to move in that direction. I called Laurel Land, and on Thursday at 1:00, we have an appointment with a funeral director. Betty, Tracy, and I are going to a funeral home to make preparations for the end of the end. Parts of dying are like being in a thick, blinding fog. There is something out there that you feel but can't see, something out there that is searching for who is here. Suddenly, out of the fog is a piercing screech. It reaches out and tries to grab you, and you scream, "No, please, no, I don't want to go." Betty wants us to go while she is still alive. She doesn't want any of us to have to do anything when she dies. She doesn't want us to ache with sadness and pain and try to make decisions about her, for her. She wants to make the decisions and have them made when we are in control of something. She says, "You will be too upset and think that everything has to be wonderful or the best. It is hard to make decisions when you are so sad and full of emotions, so let's go ahead and get this over with." No, but stop. I don't want to get this over with.*

*We will go and do this. You know what? Lots of focus is on getting there and not after, like I didn't think the funeral would be here if she was to be buried in Colorado. I thought all would be done there. So then what? What do we do? How do we get her to Colorado? There's a lot we don't know, and the things you don't know, you need to learn.*

# Chapter 28

*Thursday, February 6th, 1992*

*Hey Jean,*

It is all the way to Thursday, *two days later,* at 5:30 p.m. how are you doing? I feel so out of my life that asking you how you are seems unreal, something. I hope you're doing well and things are pleasant for you often. If there is anything I can help with, let me know. *At the beginning of the week, Wednesday, February 12th, was a long way off. Now, it doesn't seem so far. I'm not sure that if I had left on the 8th, the things we were working on would have been worked out. It is only today that some things seem to be getting done. Plenty of things to finish up over the next five days. All the heavy stuff seems to be getting in place. So maybe it will be nice and relaxing to hang out for a while before I have to leave.*

*I will miss you guys longer until I get home. I heard your voice on the tape last night, and it makes me miss being with you. It will be nice to get home. I look forward to it. I think you have been especially wonderful during these weeks and amazingly accepting. Good for you and me. Thank you!*

*Yesterday was okay. I had a telephone interview with Social Security, and then today, only 24 hours later, in the mail, I received a big package of forms that, although I haven't looked yet, promise to be long and time-consuming. I wonder who SS knows to get mail delivered in 24 hours. So, I hope to knock out these forms and applications soon.*

*Later, Betty and I had lunch with Harry. He had a good story to tell from a recent trip to New York. He rented a car, and at night, he parked near the hotel where he was staying. During the night, the attendant was distracted by a loud noise from the far corner of the lot. He went to investigate the mysterious noise, and while he was gone, someone, possibly a buddy, went into the booth and stole Harry's rent-a-car keys, and they drove off in Harry's Rent-A-Car. Luckily, it was on his American Express card, so it was covered and he won't have to pay for the stolen 1992 Chevrolet. With no car, Harry had to walk and take the subway.*

*Apparently not many cabs like to venture into Jamaica, New York. As he was walking, six youths approached him and asked for a donation to the Jamaican Boys Club. Very generously, he offered $20, but they said it was not enough. They took $80 and left Harry with nothing, and still he had miles to go on his journey. It was a good lunch, easy company.*

*After lunch, we tried our third store for the wool for the Afghan, but again it was not what she wanted. Betty is funny. I love her and love to be with her. She never sees the things that are in her way.*

*Then at 3:30 was our meeting with AIDS Interface, but you know what? It is not Interface, the big link up. It is Interfaith, the Big Link Up, it was religious. Betty and I were both pretty surprised to find out who we were really meeting with, and we began to wonder what's going on. To a degree, Betty doesn't have a lot of faith. It left her alone along the way, or she left it. The meeting seemed to work out okay, and Betty agreed to meet with two volunteers to see if she would like for them to come to the house and support her. We'll see what happens. The volunteers would come and provide emotional support, light housekeeping, short errands, and such stuff. I think it sounds good, but who knows? Betty wants to be with us; she loves us, and we will always be there. All of us will be there to do what she needs to be done. You can't miss this. There's also another group that offers buddies during times, and we will try to contact them.*

*Betty's friend Tina is supposed to get something going at work, and someone would stop by once a week to see if anything needs to be done. Betty is opening up to some of this. She's also trying to be nice and show her gratitude to everyone for their effort and kindness. I think sometimes she just goes along and says she will try something, and then when I leave she will cancel everything, and her, Tracy, and Ally will hang out all day on her bed, and they'll be perfectly happy.*

*Interfaith started to talk to Betty, and she started to cry. The way Interfaith sees things or says things made her cry. She was crying about how fast AIDS had hit her and how much she is beginning to lose control of being able to do things. She was crying and telling John Carla that she is scared that she will be left alone, that she will not be able to take care of herself, and that no one will want to be around her to take care of her. She cries and talks to strangers. Part of it is that she wants to spare us from her pain and despair. She tells John she wants to die as she is and with dignity. She does not want to die with the horror that she sees and imagines is coming. She wants to look nice and feel nice when she dies. She says she doesn't want her children and grandchildren to be afraid of her appearance. She doesn't want to see or feel people's fear when they visit her if they don't want to be there. This is what scares her and makes her cry. She is afraid that she will lie in bed and slowly waste away to nothing, to just skin and bones, and no one will want to touch her again, and no one will want to hold her again, no one will kiss again. She does not want it to become like that; she wants it to be like it is now. She wants Emma to run into her arms. She wants Emma to rest comfortably against her, she wants Emma to hug her and kiss her. This is her life, and without this, there is no life, and she doesn't want to live. And then she stops crying. Everything got so calm, and Betty says she knows everything will work out.*

# Chapter 29

*Dear Jenny,*

*Same day. After Interfaith left we all crashed and burned for a while, fueled by Betty's thoughts. I'm not sure of words that would describe Betty's thoughts and feelings that she shared. I know how they seemed: scary, sad, unsettling. Scary and sad don't reach the magnitude. Unsettling, I don't know because afterward, things were calm, and there seemed to be clarity. There was a light in the darkness showing a way through the pain and the sadness. You can begin to see outlines of your fears in the shadows, and maybe things become more manageable. Like at some point, you can become as strong, as powerful, or able to gather what you need to fight off your fears. And beyond the fear there are glimpses of a way beyond, out of the darkness that surrounds us. There's a way. Still, the light points to death.*

*Action is an evolution of ideas. The Will, the cabin.*

*Emotions become reality. Funeral home, burial.*

*This is the second time Betty has talked about dying.*

*First to Harry and yesterday to Interfaith and God. Not sure how it fits for them. Betty isn't looking for acknowledgement or acceptance of her thoughts. It's a notification of what she is going to do. I've heard what Betty wants twice.*

*Today, Tracy and I went to the funeral home. It's Sparkman Crane. Your dad was there, as were friends of Tracy and Ally. Betty was going to come with us, and last night, she was talking to Laurie on the phone. Laurie said something to her about not going, and just as easy and with a lot of relief, Betty said okay and stayed home. Probably just like it was supposed to be. Tracy and I went.*

*I've been in this place before, but until now, I've never really been inside Sparkman. It seems different. The focus sort of remains the same. The reason for being there changes. Betty is what makes it different.*

*Inside, it was very quiet. Even when there was movement, it made no sound. It seemed like it should have been dark, but it was bright, from the darkness to the light inside. The people inside didn't seem to move. They made no hand gestures. Their arms were either at their side or behind their back. No steps, quietly they floated across the room. These were the intermediates, the Directors, the people who moved you between life and death. Our Director was Ken Davis. Very nice man. I don't think he could have been anything else. He seemed to have been born for this position. He really, really seemed to care, how we felt mattered to him. He had a different insight into life and death. He's part of a transition to what you suppose or what you believe comes next. I don't suppose much. It must be different according to what people believe in. I don't know. I think death ends this life and your spirit lives on. And when you die, how will the spirit you leave be? Will it be pleasant, kind, a joy to be with, or will the spirit you leave continue to torment, bring gloom.*

*Ken knows what he is doing. He can feel the level of grief. He brought the right amount of everything. There were so many things to consider. We began with when, which we didn't know. Then considerations about viewing, rosaries, and masses. We looked at cards, announcements, and crosses. Ken will need to know what Betty will be wearing, as well as her hair and makeup. It's a bit surreal and it was this much bigger, l————————l than you would think. Makes your head spin trying to make decisions, and golly, Betty was right. It would have been incredible, unreal, trying to do this right after she died. We felt glad to be here. There was a lightness to it before death dims it. Then Ken warned us about what was next. As he solemnly led us down a short hall, "It's an empty room," he said. "An empty room filled with caskets." There were 16 different caskets, eight on each side, empty. There were metal and wood caskets, different colors of caskets, and different woodwork. They were all the same sizes. We stood quietly in the casket room, splashes and waves of sadness knocking up against us.*

*We did what we did and made many good decisions about the last time that we will see Betty. What a deal! Same thing. You have to be there before you know what it is like. We brought up about Betty being buried in Colorado, and Ken will make all the arrangements with planes, trains, and automobiles to get Betty from here to Denver and to her final place.*

*It worked without us really ever knowing how it would work. It all went well, and Betty was relieved when we got home. She was happy to see us. She was happy that we were okay, she was worried. She gave us each a hug and held us forever. She didn't want to know any of the specifics, didn't want to know the size, color or how many of anything. She wasn't interested in the price. None of that mattered to her. All that mattered was that it was done, and we were home. It's all pretty amazing. If we weren't burdened with the sadness of everything and the situation, things would be so nice. But then... So now we have a couple of days to think about a few things, and we told Ken that we would be back on Tuesday to finalize things.*

*We wind down. Betty is very happy with herself and very pleased that things are working out how she wants them to work out.*

*Good night, and I will see you soon. Tell the girls I love them, miss them, and will see them soon, too.*


*Love, Wayne*

# Chapter 30

*Friday, February 7th, 1992*

*Dear Jenny,*

*Today looks like it may be the first day in a while to sit in the backyard. It has been either rainy or cold the last couple of days. It's nice to see the sun lying across the den floor and up the walls.*

*Not much is going on here. Betty has been sitting in the den. She sits with her elbows on her knees, her arms holding up her head in her hands. She looks down at seemingly nothing. She must see something. She becomes quiet and transfixed on whatever it is that is there. What do you think she sees? It's hard for her, the sadness of dying, being so sick. She's sad for her kids, she is sad for herself, she is afraid of the pain, afraid of the dying.*

*What does it mean to have a purpose in life? Is purpose something you strive to do, something you work toward? Is purpose the result of your actions? It seems you live your life with a purpose, not sure when or if it is defined. Does the purpose of your life change when you are dying? If I sat on Old Faithful and the experiences and the things you do in life pushes you up and up and up and you bobble around on all these experiences and endless pursuits trying to get your feet on the ground. And from up here you can see what really matters, and you see what you're left with. What must that be like? To see your life in terms of a day, see your life in terms of the end. You can stop and see what you do well and define it in terms of your purpose. I can make people feel good about themselves, I can give hope to the hopeless, I can love, I can smile at someone.*

*I did that on purpose.*

# Chapter 31

*Jenny,*

*I wanted to write and say good night. How is your Friday night? You enjoy?*

*I wonder how long someone could stay on the top of a hill screaming.*

*Later.*

*Part of the day I was in my room talking through the wall to Betty. She was taking a bath. She was asking why it was worth living her life like this? Why should she live? She thinks she had a pretty wonderful life, and now to live like this seems to take away the wonderfulness of life. It's sort of weird you live your whole life and then you ask yourself why is it worth living? Betty wanted to know why she should live? Why get up and take a bath? Why have a day without tomorrow? Why live with no strength and no energy to do anything? Why live in pain?*

*What do you think why? Do you want to be alive if you can't get out of bed? Or you are in tremendous pain, or you can't bathe or feed yourself? Do you want to be alive if you're skin and bones? If people are cleaning you? Do you want to live like that?*

*There may be reasons that make sense to the living but make no sense to the dying, make no sense to her. I told her that yesterday was special and maybe that that makes it worth living another day. Yesterday Betty told Corey how well he had grown up, she told Corey that she was very proud of him and that she loved him very much. This is very special for Corey to hear this from Grandma Betty. You could see it in his face and hear it in his voice how much it meant to him and how special it was for him and through the wall I could hear Betty sniffling back tears. It makes her happy. She's the only one who could have touched Corey's heart like that.*

*And you want to try to hang on to what people give you.*

*I saw Betty again today, her head was buried in her hands. I asked her what she was doing and she said nothing. I wanted to cry. I wanted to tell her last night I was dreaming, I was afraid and please not to leave. I was dreaming that my tooth fell out. I asked Betty to stay with me till I fell asleep, and she said she wouldn't leave. Please don't leave, I said.*

*I saw Big Mike hold Betty tonight for the first time since I have been here. She melted in his hug, and she cried, then he started to cry, and they held each other crying. What's in that embrace?*

*I love Betty as a mother. Being around her I feel continually born from her. I dreamt about being young again and saw Betty as a younger mother as vividly as I see her now. She was such a big part of our lives and lived her life with us. She grew up while we grew up. It's good to be around Betty. There are times when she's so soft, warm, and quiet that she can relax. There are times when she finds a peace and calmness, and it melts away into her heart, and if you follow, it's beautiful. Inside her heart, there is a tremendous amount of love. There is kindness, caring, and desire. Inside, is how she really feels. The heart is a soft beating. The more heart you have, the stronger the beat, the glow radiates out, transcends the body and with it you can touch people, you can warm their own hearts, watch, I'm going to do it. Did it. And then there are other times she gets in such a state of hurry, impatience and aggressiveness. We all do and it causes us to lose sight of the purpose.*

*I am so grateful to be here.*

*I wonder how hard it is for Betty to feel love and compassion? Don't you think that it's a little hard to find it in there between AIDS, pain, sadness, and fear? Although it's been there most of her life, we've seen it. There are other people in the same situation, or worser. So how do they do it? Seems you have to believe in something in order to find your way. That same kid from the edge, we were at this place, inside it is total, utter darkness, all you can see is black darkness. The darkness swallowed all light, the light from the kid got dimmer and dimmer and right before the darkness swallowed the kid, we collided and held on. There were walls, and the walls brought some sense or comfort, you could reach out and touch something. What if there were no walls to hold you up? Total black darkness, and it's endless. You have to believe you will make it out, and you have to believe in something that will help you through it all, something or someone.*

*And then there is a bookmark that says, 'To love, you must love yourself' That's gotta be hard. Being able to embrace yourself, love yourself, I wonder if it is the natural state to love yourself during your life, no, the moment you die, maybe, that'd be nice, your last moments you reach out with love and at the same last moments you feel love, very nice, and you did it all by yourself. What an incredible unbelievable turmoil dying can bring with it. Maybe not. It's brought it to us, this is the beginning. It's a wild beginning, the end will be better. How do you end a life after everything you do, relationships, jobs, raising kids, vacations, all these things we do in life, all the wonderful things must stay. You could sit quietly with someone, you could hug someone, you love someone. We are able to move a glow from our hearts to someone else. How do you do all these wonderful lifetime memories, and then you die, a death outside of the norm and you become remembered not for your life but for your death. What if your death defines your life more than your life. There are heroes.*

*Hello, it is much later now, 10:30 p.m., Saturday night. I look back on this long day, and it turned out to be decent. I was thinking that this trip could be about some things about us. Maybe we could sit together,* *walk, somehow be together and look at parts of our relationship. We need some adjusting or changing to where we are now as individuals and as a couple. Maybe not really being about change or expecting change, because I don't think I can change that much. We are who and how we are. Maybe it's more about how we deal with the moments. In our conversations, they lead to some point of conflict, or even a minor irritation that gets us to where we interact against each other. We deal with one another with no room for how we areWe give each other no room to make a mistake, if either of us is wrong, it's like feeding time, and we make everything wrong, the marriage wrong. When we respond to each other it's like two wrongs make it right. It is my bam toward you, and then your Bam right back at me and then everything crumbles. You know? I don't expect my b******* to be met with loving kindness, but there has to be a little more softness when we respond to each other. If I'm an ass, don't be a bitch, and if you are, I won't be an ass. Let us have bad days, but our marriage still be based upon loving each other. Have love define our relationship. We don't want to stay like this, it will break. We have gone this far, and we need to see where we have been,* *what works, and where we can go. We both need somewhere in our marriage to be easier. Easier where we are comfortable doing whatever we are doing, either alone or together. So many factors are part of a marriage it's hard to sort through.*

*Betty signed her Will. The lawyer came this morning with a notary public who drinks Dr Pepper when she notarizes at 8:00 a.m. You don't see many of them anymore, and the big tornado hairdo too. The Will was an evolution, evolving into its final form like an artist and pleases everyone. Betty was beautiful doing the Will. There were conversations, moving and mixing numbers and ideas, hearing all the time what Betty wanted to do. I believe wholeheartedly that when a need was met, Betty loved each of her children to the utmost. They all meant to Betty the love between a mother and a child. I have heard Betty tell loving stories about each of us and in each story she would talk with a depth of sadness when any of her kids were hurt or when any of her kids were sad or scared. She would have the same strong motherly love for each and there is no one who meant more to her besides that particular child who at the time needed her. All her attention, energy, love, and money would be focused on who needed what, no one meant more to her besides that kid and she would do anything, absolutely anything if any of us were in need. She was always there.*

*It is 11:00 p.m., the Opening Ceremony of the Olympics.*

*Sweet dreams, I love you. Wayne*

# Chapter 32

*Sunday, February 9th, 1992*

*Dear Jean,*

*I was driving home from Little Tommy's second birthday and I have forgotten what I was thinking about, it was good. The second birthday party was good too. I spoke mostly to strangers or little kids. The kids running around Dallas are younger, and the adults interact mostly with adults and sometimes someone seemingly misses the enthusiasm for life that kids bring. I like Denver, it is not as hard. Katie and Mark seem to be doing okay. A point of conflict for them may be Katie's zest, which has mellowed to be more in line with Mark's dire straits. But what do I know, and who is to say?*

*Betty and Mike spent some nice time together over the weekend. She wants to spend more time with him, somehow she wants to, and he thinks she doesn't want to be with him. I wonder what kind of wall of things are between them? But if there were pictures on the* wall many of the pictures would be really good and enjoyable fun times. They do seem to be hanging around each other, somewhat casually, with all that has been bestowed upon them. Sounds like fantasy.

I feel like I want to talk to Betty. I want to tell her what she has meant to me. The reason I am here is her, her because she is sick, and her because that is what I am like from her. I want to tell her I will miss her, I will lose a lot when Betty is gone, and it's going to be hard to find it.

Bless Betty. She sits on the edge of her bed, on the edge of the couch, on the edge of the chair, she sits on the edge with her head in her hands and she wonders.

It won't be like this again. Each time I'm here with Betty it will look different, it will be different. She can feel it too, like it is happening and it's too fast. It will be what it becomes.

Well, I got to go somewhere. I like Sundays, the whole idea of resting, just one day a week everyone rests and stops what we're always doing.

Love Wayne

# Chapter 33

*Monday, February 10th, 1992*

*Dear Jenny,*

*It is Monday night, bedtime night, and tomorrow is my last day in Dallas. Today was hardly planned but it seemed to have happened like it was supposed to. I didn't plan it. I was on top and it rolled along. Top is the word backwards. The most important stuff is taken care of and we dealt with other little things that popped up. So, for parts of my last day, I'm going to do the following:*

*-pension check from Presbyterian*

*-pay Funeral Home and make changes*

*-pay bills,*

*-pay or figure out doctor bills*

*-put the Will in safe deposit box*

*-make a filing system for Betty to put mail*

*-make a phone list for er #, friends, pharmacy, places,*

*drs*

*-file a power of attorney*

*-find out about insurance*

*-Ally's car*

*Not a bad list, all of these things have been on their way to being complete or really close. Everyone has been working on this stuff all month. Hopefully tomorrow we will be finished.*

*I also need to go by Mike Leonard's to return a jacket he lent me and thank him. After 25 years, Mike and Wild Bill, I have known longer, and regardless of when, why, or how often, I can call on a groomsmen and they will be there. Doesn't matter if we don't talk for 5 years, it will be like it was yesterday. Nothing matters that can get in the way. It is never worn out and, so why not? Not sure why not. You know?*

*I have a pretty good feeling about leaving Dallas. Everything or many things are done, settled or talked about. It has been 5 weeks, we've come a long way. And it seems a lot of it happened because we had no choice, we needed to get it done, everything needs to be in place. You can't make it on your own. You gotta get help. You have to find out everything and then the more you know, the more choices you have and the easier for things to work out. It also helped that Betty knew what was going on. She knew what to do, what she wanted, she guided us, something guided us. And then BAM, over a hundred things, big things, little things, huge things came together. It worked out because it was going to as long as we did our part and as long as we followed Betty. It has been great, from the very first night in the dimly lit hallways and room.*

*Many things have happened that are going to make some sort of difference.*

*And the time I spent with Betty was incredible, unreal. I saw her pain and her sadness, her love and her beauty. It was amazing. I wish she would let me take her picture because she looks so absolutely beautiful right now. Her face, her eyes, her hair, everything is beautiful, It's got to be heaven. Where else would you be?*

*We'll take care, I will see you again soon.*

*Wayne*

# Chapter 34

*Tuesday, February 11th, 1992*

*Jean,*

*Geez, I was thinking about coming home or being home. It is almost like a vacation here. I'm a little weird about no job, nervous, and concerned about the change from here to there. It may take a couple of days to settle down. We can stay in bed.*

*Big Mike and Betty are getting along pretty well. Their relationship makes me wonder who is who and what is up with it? They're doing well, she really wants Big Mike around her. Each time I left for a while, they would come together and do things, just being around each other, and I think it will continue.*

*Do you wonder why Betty wants Big Mike around her? It must be hard for them. They loved each other, they were lovers and they want to love each other now. Maybe it's a different kind of love they have. There's no future in it, still it's there. Betty wants and needs to be loved, a love that is nurturing, a love that is gentle and soft when it smothers her she will hardly feel it. I think there are different kinds of love or different loving relationships, and the love between a mother and a child, it's your best chance. There's no love that is sweeter.*

*It seems that Betty has been becoming sick during the past 2 years, and at each time she's as healthy as she will get and the wonder of it all is how long you can be sick like this. Do you think these thoughts are necessary? I wonder how often we deal with, or think about things, certain things. How many times have I wondered about Betty's impending death? I wonder if this is what Jeff means when he says that we will talk her this way if this is what we talk about.*

*I'm glad that I'm coming home. I'm glad that I was here. See you in 12 hours.*

*Wayne*

# Chapter 35

*Wednesday, February 12th, 1992*

*Jean, I had to write during the takeoff as I was venturing back to Dallas, no it's Denver now I'll be. Many things seem to be going my way and others the wrong way. Although I have no job, or am in between jobs/careers and Betty is sick and we are where we are, how exactly are things going 'my way'? I don't know, just feels that way. There is stuff that is there, it still feels okay, or it feels as if there are other things inside of those things that are better than the outside. What it may look like is not exactly how it is, part of these things are better. I don't know. Things seem all right. I'm sitting in the second to last row, in front of me is an exit row so I have a lot of legroom. As we ascend I can see over everyone's head in front of me, all the way up to the front of the cabin and the pilot's door. I guess whether you are ascending or descending, if you are in the back you can see over everyone else. Right? The clouds are making for a bumpy ride. I guess when I get back to Denver I'm going to cool it for a while. I am out there with stuff, and there's enough movement everywhere where I can leave it and see where it goes. I guess it mostly has to do with Betty, maybe not enough movement with you and I. Definitely not enough with my job situation. I don't know what to do.*

*I just got my snack on Sun Country Airlines. It is all wrapped up in plastic, the stewardess is able to carry 25 sandwich snacks at once. The snack was okay, but it was hard to open. The stewardess told me that it was childproof and opened it for me. The four little items that made up the snack were each glued to a pink styrofoam plate. The guy sitting next to me in the window seat works for a church. It sounds like he may be a preacher, God no. He wore a cowboy hat and cowboy boots. He just seemed a bit weird. That was before he started talking to me, then it was weirder. When he was talking it's almost like I wasn't there, because who would say these things to a complete stranger? He told me that he thinks his wife is having an affair with the hippie carpenter who is redoing their kitchen. It was so weird. Now he seems to be having problems, not me. I think of all the situations in the whole world that would be the hardest and the worst* *to be in, your spouse is having an affair. Your wife or husband is with someone else. Having a wonderful, beautiful time, running into each other's arms? Can you imagine? Fear and jealousy. It paralyzes you. You can't go to work, you can't get up off the couch, you just sit there and wonder where she is, what is she doing and you rack your brain thinking it is better for her without you. No, no, no, please no. Makes you weird. You show up in strange situations wishing that you were home racking your brain instead. And then the cowboy preacher did the weirdest f****** thing, he told the stewardess that he and I were talking about her and wondering how many boyfriends she must have in each city. I swear to God, this was so nuts. I felt so stupid sitting there next to him. I started smacking his stupid head with my stupid pink styrofoam snack tray. When he got up to go to the bathroom, I got up, apologized to the stewardess, told her that I said no such thing and as I sat down feeling better about myself, it is only a matter of degrees that we are all different, still those degrees do matter, a lot.*

*Well, we have to be more than halfway there. I feel comfortable leaving Dallas as it is. I also hope something will happen between us. The magic, romance, truth, love and compassion. We all want to be in love with someone, one person.*

*I will see you soon, hope we find something there.*

*Wayne.*

# Chapter 36

*Thursday, June, 1992*

*Dear Jenny,*

*Wow, I'm back here and it is rather late after a long day. I wish I was where I am and it was 8:00 p.m. rather than 10:30 p.m. I want two more hours. I've started reading a David Eddings book, Book One of the Belgariad, Pawn of Prophecy. I am babysitting tonight, Ryan, Nick, Leslie, Tess, Daniel, Max, the little one they call Spike and the new kid. After a big spaghetti dinner we went to 7-Eleven for ice cream and then over to Ally's neighborhood pool. How fun would it be to hang out during the summer at a neighborhood pool? All the people and the kids running around, you could get to know people, lots of people, and hang out. My white body shines brighter than the sun. When I walk around I feel like my body is a beacon of bright white light. It is so hot, last night on the news the weatherman said that this weekend we would hit the century mark. What the heck does that mean? I can't wait. Today was 95°, makes me dizzy. I walk around dizzy all day. Walking into air conditioning is like an igloo, driving in the car is like being in a baked potato. If the car sits in the parking lot, you literally heat up then roast and turn red, until the AC kicks in. The pool is a lot of fun. Tess is trying hard to learn to swim, she sort of mouthed off, put her foot in her mouth and had to go down the slide. She went down really 1 fast and you could see her face freeze in the heat and panic. She was scared coming down but nothing compared to how scared she was when she hit the water and went down under. She didn't stop, later in the day she climbed up the ladder, she got to the top, had a look around and saw a huge ocean so she came down the ladder and said she would try it again later. Now she'll do just about anything. Ryan is a good swimmer, she dives off the board and goes down the slide every which way. Ryan plays real well with everyone.*

*While we were swimming, Ally was having a baby shower for a friend. At the shower, there was a lady from Ursuline who went to school with you. After the swimming Tess went home with Tracy, and Nick came home with Ryan and me. On the news I heard James King was acquitted in Denver for killing for bank cards at United Bank. I can't believe it. It is past 11:00 p.m., I'm so tired, so I'm gonna head to bed. Let me know how things are in Denver. I'd love for it to rain here.*

*Take care, see you soon, love Wayne.*

# Chapter 37

*Friday, June 19th, 1992*

*Dear Jenny,*

*Just watched the preview for "Cape Fear", pretty heavy stuff, with your favorite actor.*

*I am getting ready to watch "Backdraft". It is about 10:00, Friday night. Ryan is spending the night at Rachel's. I just tried to call to say good night and there's no answer. That's a drag because she was tired when I left her here at 5:00, and they roll long and late. Tess is in the back room coloring with Leslie. Leslie is Big Mike's youngest daughter, cute kid. Betty is in bed and Mike is in Kerrville.*

*The weather report for today was a high of 95°, then they have a type of wind chill factor for the heat and that made it 102° outside. That is incredible. The belt* on the Mercedes is loose so I drive around with the windows down acting like I like the fresh f****** burning air blowing torment around me. Today I walked on the sidewalk with no shoes and I burned my feet.

# Chapter 38

*Sunday, June 20th, 1992*

*Hey,*

*It is much later now, 5:30 p.m. Saturday, and it was a long day. I guess I'm glad to be home and that it is fairly early. Ryan and Tess are in the backroom watching T2 with Leslie. Betty is sleeping, she's spent the day in bed, the heat is tremendous for her. making her very tired, zaps her energy and she becomes very uncomfortable. My morning ended in a huge bust after I snapped a cast iron bracket that holds the flywheel to the alternator??*

*After 2 and 1/2 hours of working on the car, I was finally just about to get it done. I had replaced a fan belt that was the third belt behind two other belts that had to come off first. This I did and I was putting everything back together then snap, shit, broken, screwed.*

*Fuck it. I left, and took Ally on an extended excursion. We went to Toys R Us, Clothes R Us, Autohaus, Tracy's, Katie's, dropped Ally off at her house, then went to Braum's Ice Cream and back to Betty's where I am now. That's a very long day running around.*

*How about you? How are you? What are things like in Denver? The other day on the news I saw that you guys were going to get rain, which sounds good this time of year for the garden. It was raining here last night, the lightning woke me up, it was very loud and crashing someplace nearby, as if it was angry.*

*The kids are doing pretty well. I think they are both happy to be where they are right now, just here, alone and resting. Tess is a little sunburned and I really need to be careful because it could get pretty bad. She is going to swim with a t-shirt over her bathing suit to protect her shoulders and back. The mosquitoes too have been bad, they're big and out for blood. I have to spray Tess with Off and put Chigger-X on her bites that are spotty and splotching her body. In my fanny pack is Off, Chigger-X, Calamine Lotion, Sunscreen, Lipper, and Band-Aids, all essential items in order to survive in Dallas. A small arsenal against the elements. Ryan is doing pretty well, everyone likes to be with Ryan. There are always a lot of kids around, Ryan, Nick, Ben, Max, Tess, Daniel, Blake, Tom Tom, Emily, new kid, Leslie. Tom Tom, can you imagine he is big. Like Honey I Blew Up The Baby. Very cute.*

*Please if I get a job or even a call let me know. Briceson and Amy were at Katie's? I've never understood them together, and they still are, do you?*

*Later. Hey, I'm sitting on the couch, Tess is doing a puzzle of a colorful zebra fish swimming in green and yellow water. I wish I was swimming in green and yellow water, because if I was, I would have to be out there and I wish I was out there on top. Ryan is making Betty Crocker Supreme Dessert Bar Mix Chocolate Peanut Butter with Reese's Peanut Butter Chips. I had to ask for this twice in the store today. I'm reading Agatha Christie's Mousetrap, which is the longest running play, remember when we saw it in London? Pretty amazing that we're in London and the things we did, wow, it's like another time.*

*Tomorrow is Sunday and we are going to rest.*

# **Chapter 39**

*Sunday, June 21st, 1992*

*Dear Jenny,*

*Today is Sunday. I am sitting in the backyard. It's amazing that the trees, bushes, grass, all stay green with the heat in Texas. It is an overcast morning and I'm going to stay that way too. It will only be 88°. The plan is really to do nothing except read.*

*Later. I finished the book "Mousetrap", it was fun to read. I remembered some of the scenes from when we saw it. The day has been pretty nice. Betty has been in bed all of this day too. She really hasn't felt that well. Her energy seems to be low and she doesn't much want to do anything. All her blood work comes out good. The test shows that the CMV is not spreading. Maybe they know how to slow the infection down or knock it into remission. Even so, however it is, Betty does not feel well and no one knows why or what is wrong with her.*

*We hung out around the house reading until around 4:00 p.m. and then went over to Tracy's. I was helping Tess learn how to ride a bike, she is not too interested in learning and may break Kitt's record. I think Kitt was in her teens. It's about what the new kid was too. This bike was smaller and she was able to touch the ground while sitting on the seat, my bike at home may be too big for her to learn on. She did okay, cute kid, she has a way about her that gets her what she wants. I put training wheels on the bike and she did better and started to get a feel for it. It requires a lot of patience to teach a kid how to learn how to ride a bike, although I bet nothing compares to teaching them how to drive.*

*Tomorrow the kids start vacation bible school from 9:00 a.m. till noon. I hope they like it all right, 3 hours a day will be good for them. Why do people say that, "it will be good for you" it may not, it's off the cuff, or we think we've heard it, so we say it, dumb. All the kids are going together, Tracy's and Ally's they'll all be*

146

*there. We also go to a Ranger game tomorrow night, it is t-shirt night. The Rangers are playing the Blue Jays.*

*We'll take care. I miss you and love you. Wayne.*

# Chapter 40

*Monday, June 22nd, 1992*

*Dear Jenny,*

*It's early Monday morning, the girls should be home in a minute from Vacation Bible School. There were a lot of kids there this morning, hundreds of them. The place was so big and there were just as many volunteers as there were kids. There were six women working in Tess and Daniel's class. Ryan is with Nick, Ben and Corey. We'll see how it all goes. When they get home I'm going to go by travel agents and also find a place for Tessa's birthday party. Tonight is a Ranger game, Tess does not want to go so she will stay here at Betty's with somebody.*

# Chapter 41

*Tuesday, June 23rd, 1992*

*Dear Jean,*

*I'm sitting at the end of eight red chairs, occupied by 7 6th graders and me. It is quiet time at Vacation Bible School, everyone's head is bowed. I am writing under my coat. I'm here to pick everyone up and I just walked through the middle of a power lunch at the church. A lot of action going on in this church. Quiet time just ended and now all the kids are up, laughing and running out the door. See you later.*

*Oh Jean I feel so hot, I wish you were here. My insides, my outsides, behind sides, my head and my feet, everything is so hot. I feel like I need to take it easy. We were at the pool from 1:30 to 4:30. The wind chill factor was 103°. We were playing volleyball, and a little girl burned her feet in the sand. Ally is home sick to her stomach, Lauren is pink, Ryan and Tess survived. The heat is crazy. Tess wore a t-shirt all day and hasn't had too much problem with sunburn or the huge mosquitoes. Later, wayne.*

# Chapter 42

*Wednesday, June 25th, 1992*

*Dear Jenny,*

*Good morning, how is it in Denver? I noticed again that it was going to be hot there. Are you staying busy? I was thinking about you after you called last night. It's cool what distance does to thoughts and feelings, at times it offers the best potential to what is already there.*

*I am at CCC right now. Betty got a call this morning that the results from her blood test yesterday require that she have a small blood transfusion tomorrow, three units of blood. We are here today for some prep work. The tests have shown that she is doing well, her blood has been good and her CMV is dormant for the most part. On the other hand I have been here for almost 6 days and Betty has been in bed for four plus today will be five of the days in bed.days On the seventh day she will have an 8 hour blood transfusion. There is a lot of learning going on to how to treat AIDS. It is not a science, the treatment is being developed, it's not there, stopping HIV, it can't be done, a cure, no, none of this is there yet. They don't have the answers. Ask your questions all you want and there are no answers. Absolutely they are working hard, research, development, it's all going on. They will find a treatment, a cure, they always have. So it's really hard to access her health, everything goes up and it all comes crashing down, making you dizzy and confused.*

*Home at last. I'm on the couch. My feet are extended outward, my back resting comfortably on the big pillows.*

*The blood transfusion is due to the medicine AZT. The AZT is destroying Betty's red blood cells. AZT is an antiviral medicine. One of the side effects is that it destroys red blood cells. Red blood cells supply your body with oxygen, and the loss of oxygen leads to anemia, you get tired and weak. And that's been what is going on during the last six days. That's wild.*

*CCC is a very nice place. However Betty found her way there, it is very fortunate. Everything is so clean, the people are unreal, they are wonderful, everyone is so happy. Betty loves it here, the nurses hug her, they hold their hand and treat her like she is a princess. They adorn Betty with love and care. And they love Tracy's children. Tracy comes in carrying one baby and two other babies tagging along somewhere behind her. All the nurses fawn at the kids, stretching out their arms reaching for the babies and affectionately hugging them to their chest. All the Oooz and Aahs, everyone is so cute and wonderful, like in a feel good movie you dream of being a part of.*

*Golly what can it be with no insurance, the lines, the waiting, people all around who are sick and tired of AIDS. It would be awful and I'm sorry.*

*Dale is a nurse and seems to be the manager of CCC.*

*He is a great guy, he radiates kindness and caring, he is so nice to everyone. I say everyone, because Tracy and Betty laugh and tease me, and another nurse told Betty I was gorgeous. Funny world.*

*See you later, Wayne*

# Chapter 43

*Thursday, June 25th 1992*

*Dear Jean,*

*It is almost 10:00 a.m. I'm reading two posters in the waiting room at CCC. There is an HIV class going on in the back. A patient with HIV is waiting for a ride home. Betty is here for her transfusion, 8 hours. I'm going to stay till about noon, then Tracy is coming with a movie to watch with Betty while she's being transfused.*

*The girls are at home, no Vacation Bible School today, they would have gone but we're okay with not going.*

*Last night we went to the Ranger game and we got home pretty late. It was raining this morning so we thought it would be a nice morning to sleep in. Ally and Corey are going over to Betty's in the morning to stay with the girls till I get home.*

*About the Ranger game. Yesterday with the wind chill factor at 112°, we raced through 5:00 Dallas traffic to get to a 7:30 p.m. baseball game. It was autographed night and Don Ross baseball card book night. We waited in line for one autograph and then we all ran to the other side of the stadium in 112° for the second autograph. And we weren't done, we ran again to the middle of the stadium for a chance to be on TV and ask a man wearing a purple shirt and purple hat a question about the Ranger's. I sure was excited. I had my question already, you know what I was going to ask them?*

*There we were me, Tracy, Ben, Corey, Ryan, Daniel and Tessa who decided at the last minute to come. Go Tess. We were at the very top of Arlington Stadium in the 112° heat, it was nuts, our faces were bright red burnt from the sun.*

*The game was really good, although Rangers lost 3-2 to Toronto, good pitching, Wells and Witt. Toronto has a good team.*

*Well I have moved from the lobby and am now sitting in Betty's room at CCC. It is a very nice clean room, painted white and gray tv, vcr, everything looks pretty normal and innocent except for the IV with a donor's blood slowly dripping into Betty. Blood is such a dark color, a red black when it is all together in a bag and then a light almost see through red when it is just a drop dripping through the line. Betty looks good, her color is good. I hope she gets a bit of a surge of energy from this, she was anemic so this will help.*

*In her head, and I guess in her heart, but that's not right, bitterness and anger don't reside in the heart. And Betty is rather bitter, angry about Big Mike's father, his son, everyone and everything it seems she's bitter toward. To what degree can you live like this, because we're all to a degree. Maybe we can mellow out about some of the things and try not to even bother with them, at this point how much does it matter, this isn't right either because I don't know all that matters and it is so easier said than done.*

*Tracy just got here with her video but Betty is about to crash on Ativan. Ativan is really weird, you go way out there. Betty won't even know who I am, or even what is wrong with her, she will want to know what she is doing here and then she will want to leave and go home hoping she will feel safer. She will see people she has never seen before, and be in places she's never been to. It really gets strange and she always gets scared because she doesn't recognize anything in her life. She gets scared because she won't know where she is, she gets zapped out to the end of the universe and it scares her so bad. It's crazy, scary and sad to see her messed up like that. These are the wonder drugs used in the 90s and people know longer have to feel anything, Ativan works in your head to try and calm down the crazy thoughts tormenting you with millions of synapses going crazy in your mind. There she goes, bye Betty. See you when you get back. Love you*

# **Chapter 44**

*Friday, June 26th, 1992*

*Dear Jenny,*

*Hours later, day's later, it is 11:00 p.m. Friday night. Ryan, Cory and I are watching Eddie Murphy, "The Golden Child." Tess is sleeping. It was nice to talk to you this evening. I miss you.*

# Chapter 45

*Sunday, June 28th, 1992*

*Hey,*

*The girls just left with your sister Bridget. I strapped them both into a fire engine red, two-door, two seater, two people, MR2. They are either on their way to Irving for fun and games at the Canal Festival or to a play about a futuristic Pinocchio in the Year 2164. When is 2164? I hope the girls are aware and appreciative for what Bridget does with them and expresses their thanks. And Bridget, with her kindness and hustle, does not always seem to be aware and appreciative of their time together. Everywhere, sea to shining sea people are like that, we know not what we do and what is right there.*

*Yesterday, the girls and I drove up to McKinney to see Harry. We went to Saturday evening mass. Then to El Chico's for dinner. El Chico's is the best, food is good, atmosphere is good, great place. After dinner we went to a park where there was a small brass band playing. It was nice. Harry seemed excited and interested in being together. When we got back to his house, Harry and I sat in the library. The library is just like you would suppose, volumes and volumes of books, hundreds of awesome metal soldiers, regiments, horse brigades, incredible detail, pictures from around the world and clocks telling time everywhere in the world. It is really quite a room. We each sat in a high back leather green chair, with a soft light between us. You come here to talk and we talked about some pretty cool things, men things. Just kidding, I know that it can be not right for men talk, girl talk is ok. I swear Harry told me stories he doesn't always share. It was cool. And why do you reckon they aren't shared?*

*Part of it was because it was men talk, adventures, exploits, conquer, intrigue and that's all good, do you think? People in a relationship have their own stuff. I don't think having your own stuff butts heads with*

*Sally saying "we love each other, so we share everything". That's great, for you. It's gotta be however it works for you and you go for that and I will do the same. What works for us.*

*Anyway, Harry showed me press releases having to do with Mr. Perot and the statement Harry is to read in a Senate Subcommittee on Tuesday. The Committee wants to know about American POWs in Vietnam. Mr Perot and Harry have done more than anyone for the American POWs. They absolutely believe and have proof. They never gave up, they never stopped looking, they followed every lead, into jungles, villages. They were God's gift for the search for Americans. And their humility would never expose what these two great men did. Once on the river bank of the Mekong River, with thousands of dollars to exchange for an American POW. It didn't work, they didn't stop. Harry did some incredible things, Braniff planes to Vietnam POWs, the logistics for Spirit Of Texas, the EDS hostage rescue, Jesse Jackson meeting the Pope, all humble*

*Harry.*

*The girls and I slept upstairs in the newly renovated attic space. What a space. It is like all the trains you can have in one space. A train collection includes about 25 locomotives and another 200 mostly Lionel trains. Trains from around the world, mostly the major U.S. lines and old NYC subway cars. The track goes around the perimeter of the room on the floor, it's one big open room, it's gotta be 1200 sq ft. Then the locomotive pulling five Amtrak cars winds around the chimney that's just off the center of the room. Winds four times around the chimney on a big wooden trestle. Then the track goes all around the perimeter of the room at about waist high. Pretty awe inspiring, what a collection. The big locomotive and a few other cars I recognized when growing up. There's a tie train, a red train that small ties would fall through. I always thought I bought that red train for Harry, or he let me pick it out. That's 30 years ago at least that Harry started collecting trains. The room is huge, it's a lot of track and a lot of trains. The ceiling in the room is painted with gold and dark green, the ceiling looks trainy. The decor in the room is 'leftover' from the museum pieces throughout the rest of the house. Leftovers are beautiful, unique, treasures, it's crazy. There are five Kim Means original paintings of Southwestern men and women. They are beautiful, the simplest providing such beauty and intrigue coming from the colors, the lines, the expressions, you can see so much in so little. Excellent paintings. There are also beds at different sides of the room, the distance offering some privacy. And a sort of open bath area, a folding silk screens providing privacy. It is really an interesting space, lots of things to enjoy. It rained and thundered all night, which wasn't good. I told Tess about a ghost that lives in the attic, it's the original owner. The lightning and thunder seemed to wake this old house and there were a lot of noises that kept us awake.*

*Breakfast was to be served at 8:00 a.m. but was*

*delayed until 8:40 a.m. because of the weather. I don't know.*

*After breakfast we sat around for a while and looked at pictures of Harry's recent trip to Moscow and Siberia. Why do you think Harry was in Moscow, and Siberia? Vacation? He didn't say much. There were times growing up thinking Harry did secret stuff. Harry then had to take Rebecca to the airport so we showered and we left.*

# **Chapter 46**

*Monday, June 29, 1992*

*Geez Jean, what a morning. Every time I see something it is something I have never seen before. I heard things and felt things I have never felt before. It was hard with Betty this morning. When I went into her room she was in the bathroom vomiting and wetting herself. She just barely had the strength to hold herself up over the toilet, anything less she would have been on the floor lying in a mess. It was like this all morning,*

*Betty has been sick all morning. She can't eat or drink, everything that she tries to take in makes her sick to her stomach. When she tried to take her pills earlier the water made her sick, she started to choke and gag, we moved slowly into the bathroom, like we were barely moving, she vomited more and it was painful, she was doubled over from the pain in her stomach, an intense aching. She would try and hold herself tightly in a ball, in a fetal position, that's so weird, the life cycle. It was unreal, it was not of our living world, the smell, the sounds, the images, the pain, all of it was everywhere and it was everything. It is screaming at you, I couldn't breathe anymore. I left the room.*

*I shouldn't have left. Fuck. That's exactly what Betty doesn't want, to be left alone. Fuck.*

*What do we do? I want someone to tell us what to do. What would you do? I don't know. How do we help Betty? What controls all this? Why is it like this? It's like Bam Bam Bam, it didn't seem like it was going to stop all morning. Things can be so tremendous. There's no answer to why. Maybe the questions are wrong so you won't get a right answer.*

# Chapter 47

*Hey,*

*I'm somewhere on top.*

*Hi Jenny,*

*The morning rolled into the afternoon and now it is evening. The whole day has been the same, sad. Betty would try to be up for a while in between being sick. Your being is sick.*

*Once I tried to give Betty some water. I sat her up in bed, she was unable to hold her head up. Her head would bob up and down, then jerk back up, like she had no control, she tried so hard just to get a f****** sip of water. She couldn't do it. Then her head would just lie there between her shoulders, gently swaying back and forth, like it was in the wind. I'd lift her head, hold her chin, and bring water up to her lips. A sip of water brings relief, the greatest sip of a lifetime.*

*medicine for the nauseous and then she is so messed up she can't even begin to get it. I've never been anywhere near where she goes, if I get half way there it's crazy. I hope it gets better, please get better. There's a psychosis to all of this. Can you hear the psychosis?*

*Because every time you seem to get an answer it doesn't seem to matter anymore because of what is going on, it moves so fast what's right smack in your face, and that is all that matters and it's all you can deal with. The other crazy part is fear. It's fear of what is going on every moment and it's fear of the unknown, fear of the beast that is going to kill Betty. Oh Fuck, I can't believe that I wrote that, that's terrible to say. I was wrong, it was never a beast, it was the beauty that kills Betty.*

*Betty is such a sweetheart. It comes down to her.*

*Later*

*What is going on with you? The kids are still out with your sister, remember that? Hopefully they're out of the two door, two-seater red sports car. They both have their hands full, Bridget and the girls. Thank God they're great kids. It is fun to watch Ryan, she gets real proud of herself either when I'm talking about her or when she does something. Then she starts to get a little full of herself and she'll test new waters.*

*Well Jean, I'm going to read my book, fall asleep and dream, dream about an enchanted world where all that I know does not exist as I know it, but in a world filled with its purest that flows and moves easily toward life in its most loveliest form.*

*Love Wayne*

# Chapter 48

*Monday, June 29th, 1992*

*Dear Jean,*

*It is rush hour in Dallas, can you imagine what it's like driving around here at 5:00 p.m? It's nuts. I'm sitting in the backyard.*

*Hey, right when I started this letter, Betty woke up at rush hour. I love her.*

*It's now 9:00 p.m. Betty is beginning to feel better. Maybe there is a developing pattern of how AIDS affects Betty. She gets really sick for a period of time, that time period gets longer and she gets less well afterwards, each time a little less well. There are times of intense pain and despair. When she feels better, things get quiet, and there is a calm. A calm brought about because there is nothing left,*

*everything you had, you used to deal with the period*

*of pain and despair. You ever seen the knight in shining armor after battle? He's sitting outstretched against a wall, his blood soaked sword lying at his side. Blood, pain, despair cover his face. He's exhausted, quiet, and calm. There's no reflection in the calmness, you'll automatically know what to do next time. You learn and feel things each time there is an experience. Learning is in the brain, in your head. Feelings are in your heart. That's what we want to guide us, what's in the heart.*

*Once Betty starts to feel better, she will get up and down out of bed, go back and forth from the bedroom to the den. Back and forth, up and down until she no longer knows where she is. Three hours, it was like this during the day, then she took a short rest and has now been up since 5:30 p.m. It's a long time. I wonder if while you are dying, you want to be awake, try to fill up the time that is left. But then I've seen resting and sleeping bring relief.*

*I feel more fearful of AIDS this trip, and so far it's*

*been inhibiting me somewhat when I go to Betty. Guess what had a hand in this?*

*Today I wrote, typed and mailed a letter to Phil Martinez at Englewood Public Schools. The job is at Englewood High School teaching 9th graders Economics and Civics. I am enclosing a rough draft of what I wrote. What do you think? Too Foo Foo?*

*I need to make sure that somehow I get an interview, and get the job. It would indeed be great.*

*God I missed you today. How are you? I received your letter today; it was most memorable. You mentioned missing the girls. I imagine they would be missed the most. It's hard to be away, they will be back soon, and I will be too. I'm going to read for a while. Take care, sweet dreams.*

*Love Wayne*

# Chapter 49

*Hey Jean.*

*Tuesday night. I lost my favorite pen, hence the black ink. Not too much going on today. I spent the morning cleaning up the garage so I can park the Mercedes in it.*

*I went birthday shopping for Tess but couldn't find anything. Tomorrow I'm going to Toys R Us. I reserved a party at Jungle Gyms. It is like the place in Denver where Tess wanted to have her party. This place has a lot more rides. Tess is inviting Blake, Lauren, Daniel, Max, Ryan, a new kid, and Spike.*

*We went to CCC for Betty's dressing change. We told CCC how sick Betty has been, they took some blood samples and we'll see if any adjustments need to be made with something. I'd say so. Betty has been up since 1:00 this afternoon and she's very tired. Sometimes when Betty gets tired and is resting, she will start to talk. Today she said that she has done everything she wanted to do in her life, she said she was content and she believes that she has lived a very good long life. She seems to think that her age is old enough to die and in these ways she is somewhat ready to die. Betty said if AIDS hadn't come along she wouldn't have thought about dying but now that it is here, she's getting ready. She's 61 years old. I don't think that is old enough, Betty does. Don't know.*

*So what else is news? Laurie said she has talked to Ralph about moving to Denver. We'll see. They could always stay with us for a bit until they find a place. It'd be wild, Laurie. How are the flowers along the fence with Ken looking? How about the veggies along the back fence? According to the weather, it seems like it's been raining there. It's hot here. On the weather report they talk about 1980 in Dallas. That was the year I worked for Big Mike putting in sprinklers in Dallas. That year was the record year for heat. Forty two days of 100 plus degrees and Lumpy and I were the only ones outside. We were digging sprinkler trenches. We would be dropped off in the morning and Lumpy, a big friend of Big Mike's, would turn the wheelbarrow over under the shade and sit in it till we were picked up in the afternoon and I shoveled trenches. Every night I see it on the news and I'm reminded of that summer with Lumpy.*

*I'll take care, you too. I will see you soon.*

*Love Wayne*

# Chapter 50

*Wednesday, June 30th, 1992*

*Dear Jen,*

*Just spending the morning idly. Is idly a word, or is it iddly? I can't spell. I am hanging out in the backyard, a really nice breeze is shaking the tree, and big bell chimes sing out. Nicest morning yet. I just finished the last 80 pages of Book 1 of the Belgaraid, so I've been immersed in that for most of the morning. It took me about 6 days to read the first 30 pages and then three days to read the last 230 pages. They're really good books: fantasy, kings, queens, goblins, magicians and sorcerers, castles, faraway lands, enchantment, adventures, and quests.*

*"You simply will something to happen", the old man said,*

*"and then speak the word, if your will is strong enough*

*it happens.''*

*Far out. That seems like it is true. Will is composed of courage, perseverance, desire, love, if those are strong something will happen. And then like you harness that strength, then you can create, then you can make things happen. You reckon?*

*The thought to form idea. The books are fun to read and I enjoy them.*

*I got your call today about the girls getting home and when. I really haven't thought too much about it. I'll see what I can do and work something out.*

*Later...*

*Well Jenny you spurn me into action. I found a flight for the girls and will book it on the 8th of July and I will fly home on the 18th. I'll pay cash for one of the tickets and charge the other two. Our charge card will blow up to $339, drag, but unavoidable.*

*Well it is almost 1:00 p.m., I've been on the back porch with only minor interruptions since 8:30 a.m. Better go.*

*Love Wayne.*

# Chapter 51

*Thursday, June 31st, 1992*

*Dear Jenny,*

*It is another windy morning, kids are still asleep and I hope they stay like this. The wind is really blowing and then it is supposed to be a wind chill factor day of 110 °. Right now the wind is blowing bunches and bunches of big fluffy clouds from the northeast. It is almost like being at sea with the trees, chimes and clouds all blowing. It is beautiful sitting out here, it helps. Tess, I'm at sea.*

*Besides Betty's physical health going up and down, so do emotions. Everyone's emotions are out there, floating like balloons among needles, and they burst. Busted by the piercing of the pain and fear, the emotions explode all over. Fear gives rise to sadness. Fear and anger face off between each other or between her and I. It may be my fear, her anger. Or is it my anger, her fear. Emotions need their own medicine. The emotions are tied to her having to live each day with living and dying. What's the medicine for that? Polar opposite of anger and fear is compassion and truth. Compassion. Compassion and love fix things.*

*Now the wind is blowing violently against the trees, blowing the branches to their limits, blowing us past limits.*

# Chapter 52

*Wednesday, July 1st, 1992*

*Dear Jean,*

*Didn't think I would be writing this morning, but odd, idle moments are plenty in the early morning. Everyone is asleep and if you listen you can hear the silence. Sitting here in the backyard has to be the best place there is. Paradise.*

*I have been wondering about our phone conversation last night, having some random thoughts. We have thoughts or we say things that may never end up meaning anything. Thoughts that go nowhere, manifest nothing and may become destructive because they don't do anything. While we were talking, I could have been out of place, I am out of place. I was frustrated. We haven't been able to talk for any time about anything. I don't know. We each need something and it is not coming from each other, or barely from anywhere in our lives. You and I are about where we were when I left Denver. Distance isn't between us, there is stuff, issues between us, or around us and we both are out there running around and around wanting to crash into each other.*

*Love Wayne.*

# Chapter 53

*Thursday, July 2nd, 1992*

*Dear Jenny*

*Hello, we are at home after Tessa's party at Jungle Gyms. Ryan and I made a chocolate cat cake that looked like a cat. Ryan, Leslie, Daniel, Lauren, Max, Blake, and Spike came to the party.*

*You know who I saw there? Jane and Meagan and Paige, pretty wild. They stayed together, they were young when they met, they were always able to laugh and move on from things, they were cool. I was always glad they were together.*

*The birthday party was great. Everyone had a really good time and enjoyed one another. All the kids were smiling, running, holding hands, laughing. Never matters the age, holding hands is so good. Party was nice. The rides were a lot of fun, they went very fast, the kids would be spinning around, holding on tight, their breath caught inside of them. Betty was there. She'd follow the kids around to each of the rides resting on the benches. She watched the kids have fun, smiling and laughing and she could feel the same way from the kids. As they got off the rides, Betty would hug them and they would be off to the next ride and the next bench. Betty can see the things and feel the things that matter to her. We all can do this and have had experience.*

*Some are really really magical. I always understand it to be the breath that brings you into the moment, aware of the inhale and exhale that focuses you. I'm not sure Betty is using the breath. It seems the experience itself often focuses you on the wonder. Not always though. We miss a lot. Maybe sometimes there is so much going on and you are all over the place. I guess then use the breath again.*

*Betty looked good, I took her picture, she always looks good, she is so pretty and she dresses so nice. I like how she moves around and how she rests, how it is only the moment for her, it's wonderful.*

# Chapter 54

*Hello,*

*How are you? How is the holiday?*

*Friday the 3rd was cool, the afternoon and night were very nice. Big Mike, Betty and I, Tess and Leslie were at home and we had the best time lighting fireworks. They were big, they were bright, it was great, it was a wonderful experience.*

*Jeff called earlier that evening. We continued on our disagreeable, and a bit heated conversation about things, about AIDS, mostly about AIDS and Betty. Jeff has been around people with AIDS and he has seen the progression of the disease. I don't have experience, never been around it, never knew anyone. All I seem to know is what I see, what I feel each day and it is not comforting. While he was telling me that he's coming up for 24 hours to see me, Betty and Harry. Tess was on the back porch popping a small plastic baggie filled with snapper poppers. One popped, then another, then she drops some of the poppers, they fall to the ground and she steps on them they start popping, she drops the whole bag and out of a hidden corner, six little boys come running right at Tess, pushing to get the fallen popper, Tess freaks out more and screams, I yell out to Tess that everything is alright while Jeff is yelling the same to me about Betty. It's crazy. I know, you know, we all know if it's alright and what we know is different and not everyone knows the same. Shortly after this everyone left, Tracy and her four kids and Didi and her child and nephew, little Fulbrights. Later in the evening,*

*Big Mike, Betty, Leslie, Tess and I shot off some fireworks in the backyard. You would have thought we were blowing up dynamite with all the caution that was administered to Tess and Leslie using sparklers. They had to be 10 ft away using 8 ft matches to light sparklers. Betty and Mike had fun. Betty liked to watch both kids enjoy themselves with their dads. It means something. Betty is a sweetheart, a real live sweetheart, she can see the sweetest things happening. After that we drove over to Prestonwood and we watched the Addison fireworks, and it was just what Betty wanted it to be. The fireworks were excellent, they were big and bright and the finale lit up the whole sky that we could see was exploding. It was a great night.*

# Chapter 55



*Sunday, July 5, 1992*

*Hello Jenny, how are you? What you up to today? How was your 4th?*

*Ours was really, really cool. In the morning we hung out and made a 4th of July cake. Pound cake on the bottom, then a layer of blueberries and strawberries covered with whipped cream. We used more blueberries as stars and sliced strawberries as the stripes.*

*It looked just like a flag. We went over to Tracy's in the early afternoon for barbecue, volleyball, ping pong and swimming. All you can really do is swim because of the heat. Jeff was there, the Wilson's came by, Wild Billy shook more dust out… it will show you where it's at. ', Diddy and her entourage, Ally and her kids were there and Big Mike came by with Leslie. Betty spent the Fourth resting. It was a lot of fun, the food was great, burgers, dogs, chicken, lots of salads, fruit and the 4th of July cake. It was fun to see everyone, some real funny people, it was a joy in the midst. And it just got better after the party.*

*Imagine this, on the 4th of July, 1992 we went to the Ranger game that night. The Rangers versus the Yankees. Nolan Ryan was pitching on the 4th of July in America on America's Birthday, something exciting like that. It was incredible just to be there, almost like where else would you want to be? Nolan Ryan pitched a great game, 13 K's, 3 hitter. Ryan was pitching a shutout, top of the ninth inning, two outs, two strikes, 0-2 count and the batter hit a homerun. Unbelievable to watch and be there, crazy, it was a great game. That's a story to tell, you're my first,*

*I'm going to try and tell everyone. "I was at this game."*

*The whole day and night was wonderful, lots of great people, great food, great entertainment, great game, great fireworks, late night.*

# **Chapter 56**

*Tuesday, July 7, 1992*

*Hi Jenny,*

*Today wasn't a very good day. The biggest drag was not getting that job. And thinking why I didn't get the job. I thought that if I interviewed for a job, I would get it. I thought I would get the job cuz I was older, although I have the wrong experience, I was a loan officer. I have good reference letters from student teaching and subbin. At the interview I wasn't dressed right, too casual, not proper, my hair was a mess. I let them down right away when they are expecting a 36-year-old man. I need to be more of that. And I need to express energy, how do you do that? I was putting them to sleep with my long rambling answers. I had to cough twice to wake them up. Energy, they want to know the kids are going to be excited to learn, they also want you to know how you can handle the kids.*

*The assumption, there are ' kids', have discipline problems and that becomes most of the interview. They want someone that can handle the situation when it gets out of control. I use magic, it's hard to explain how it works, even if they see it, they won't see how it works.*

1.	*Look the part*

2.	*Energy*

3.	*A manhandler*

*I need to prepare answers with examples, short crisp exciting answers that don't ramble and go in circles. Like I am now. The job was mine, they wanted me, even at 7:00 p.m. the night before I was leaving town, they got together for the interview and I blew it when I showed up. S***. I need to do something. If it fell into my lap I would take it, but how it is now is fine.*

*The rest of the day was terrible. I blew a bunch of money at Sears and they didn't even fix the car. The car. I thought they could handle fixing the AC, but after they tried and failed, they told me I needed an authorized Mercedes dealer to work on the car.*

*And Jeff was here, I don't think he is too keen on the idea of buying a cabin in Colorado. But then I was confused, I couldn't tell when he was serious or messing around about stuff. So I don't know, yesterday was a drag. When I got home I was hot, broke, tired and bothered. I was supposed to go out that night but blew it off at the last minute.*

*Take care, Love you,*

# Chapter 57

*Wednesday, July 8, 1992*

*Today the girls are leaving, and I'm staying.  They had a good time here and spent time with lots of people. I will really miss them. They are diamonds among the rough, they're great kids, well behaved, mellow, fun to be, they're wonderful. They had a good time and fun to be around. They're wonderful. We did a lot together: Ranger games, movies, Wet and Wild, parties, swimming, fireworks, and puzzles. Tess has 11 completed puzzles stacked in the living room.*

*I better go and do some packing. God bless me, I love you, Miss you, sorry about the job.*

*Love Wayne*

# Chapter 58

*Saturday, July 11, 1992*

*Dear Jean,*

*There it is, Jean again, all by itself, it happens. How are things in Denver? What you guys up to today? Not much is going on here. I'm working on job stuff. I would really hate to substitute next year, it makes me lazy and broke. I subbed last year from 91-92, not again, ugh. I'm hoping to learn something from these How to Do books, this one is about interviewing. I also hope that Mary Ellen can give me a tip, I always think that she can help me, eventually maybe. She treats people like that, she delivers. My interviews are terrible; I am too monotone, too rambling, not exciting—it's dumb. I'm not projecting myself as what they are looking for, like confidence and excitement, I need to practice my questions and answers that support their expectations. I need to talk about methods and how I'm able to do something in the classroom.I need a lot, and I'm willing to listen to all suggestions.*

*Right now it's 3:15 on a hot muggy Saturday and across Dallas at 4:00, Nick and Ben play their final game of the baseball season.*

*You know about us, maybe there is more of our life together than there is, but not a lot there in between episodes and disagreement, there's something there.*

*Hey, I'm back. Right at the moment the house is full of Clarks. There are nine of them here passing through town; they are all so big, giants. Dean is the biggest, a whole doorway full of beef, and the kids are almost as big. They are all huge, and they fill everything, they fill the chairs, couches, the tables, they fill the bathroom and all the beds, they fill the whole house. The only thing not full is the fridge after all this Clark stuff. They eat everything and they will eat anything, huge helpings all at once, plates and bowl fulls, 2-3 bowls of cereal all at once. They are an amazing part of our species.*

*I will see you later, I hope it all works, I love you.*

*Love Wayne*

*PS Tell those two wonderful beautiful girls that I miss them and enjoyed every minute we had together, they are exciting spontaneous delights.*

*If you could imagine one thing in your life being like you imagine it to be, what would it be?*

# Chapter 59

*Hey Jean,*

*I'm back, it's a little after 7, and I'm settled in for the night. I'm going to write, read my book, eat ice cream, grapes and brownies. After being out I was going to cruise up to McKinney and spend the night at Harry's. I stopped by Betty's to see how she was doing and I decided to stay with her. It's an opportunity to hang out with Betty while she is enjoying something and enjoy it with her. Last night was a bit rough with a house full of Clarks, especially after Dean Clark took off his size 12 shoes and his crusty socks. He then stretched his big toes that were on his big foot, stretching them the whole length of Betty's couch. Betty watched as all this unfolded and she started to turn a crazy reddish color. Then she said some mean things to Big Mike about all those big clark toes and what she was going to do with them if she saw them on her couch again. They both got a little excited and exchanged some words, so Betty and I went out for a drive. It was nice, we talked a little bit about all the Clarks, and she very, very reluctantly decided to try to become the hostess without the mostest. It will be very hard for her. We got back and Big Mike and Betty were doing a little better. They bump up against the limits of their relationship. I guess we all do but what does that mean, limits to a relationship? Do you think there are limits, where a relationship is strained too much to carry on? Where do limits come from? Can you move past your limits? There's a poem about love and what we each have to give up coming into a relationship with someone else. What is it that we have to give up? 'Our longing for the perfect.' (Robert Bly.) There is none.*

*Betty has a reserve of anger that she will blast out there and boy you sometimes have to watch out. She tries and it is hard, she's been betrayed, never by her kids, that wasn't ever an issue, it was never part of her mothering. She loved us and she will always love us.*

*And it was easy to love Betty. She was so young. I don't know, it's crazy, so many things, not sure what I was writing about.*

*Love Wayne.*

# Chapter 60

*Sunday, July 12, 1992*

*Dear Jean,*

*Sunday morning, early. Big Mike is at church praying. Betty is sleeping back in her room. She's rested and comfortable when she sleeps. She's pretty when she's sleeping. I'm hoping for the next couple of hours, I can sit in this big comfortable chair and write to you and read. I'm on page 270 of Book Two of The Belgariad, with about 50 pages left. Then I guess I start Book Three then Four and Five. I know that because they're numbered. Book One and Two are about 600 pages of traveling and in search of an orb. Along the way they encounter lots of different people and places, and adventures.*

*I've also begun to read about Catherine the Great, Russian princess in 1770. Betty, Big Mike and I go to an exhibit at Fair Park on Wednesday at 5:00 p.m. for*

Catherine the Great. The exhibit has 300 pieces from The Hermitage Museum that Catherine had built in St Petersburg which recently was Leningrad and changed back to St Petersburg. The pieces on exhibit include a golden egg and a golden carriage, all gold, that's crazy, the rich have so much. Betty and I have been searching libraries and bookstores for information on Catherine. It's been a lot of fun. I've learned some things that have tied together history for me. Betty really enjoys royalty; she loves Princess Di.

Tracy found a little black kitten that was abandoned in her front yard. The kitten fits into the palm of your hand and barely has its eyes open. Maybe the mother left it there accidentally. Betty has been nursing it with little nipples and bottles they sell at the pet store she named the kitten Catherine.

Betty also reads Agatha Christie books that Ryan left. We saw that play too, the longest-running ever, The Mousetrap. You remember that trip. Harry was entertaining the Braniff Board and you and I tagged *along on the extras. I think it was Elaine Paige in Evita, Yul Brynner in The King and I, Hair, and The Mousetrap. Pretty incredible to see such performers and performances. It's been a nice, relaxing day.*

*Well, have a nice day. See you later. Wayne*

# **Chapter 61**

*Jenny,*

*Later it is.*

*You know people are funny. Bob has been here all day and he was here most of last evening. Bob is like a great big wild hormone. Every time I look around there is Bob and he's always laughing, and I never know what he's laughing about. Sometimes I think he's laughing at me. I always check my zipper, my nose, he's that sort of guy who would laugh at that stupid shit. Anyway, while I was taking a shower Big Mike and Bob came into my room and sprayed buckets of ammonia in my closet. There's been a big drip from the attic from the air conditioner and before anyone had noticed it, it turned the walls in my closet different shades of green mold. So Big Mike and Bob sprayed the closet with ammonia to kill the mold and me. Then they shut the door, gas trapped inside, pressure building. When I walked out of the bathroom into the bedroom, an explosion of ammonia washed over me like a wave as it overwhelmed each of my senses, my eyes watered then started burning, my skin burned, I had trouble breathing it was so incredibly strong, this much more than what you are thinking. I yell out to Big Mike, and then Bob starts falling all over the den with this wild laughter. I was confused, even Big Mike stopped to stare at Bob wondering what was going on, and then he checked his zipper. They followed me back into the bedroom Big Mike takes a big breath and almost passes out, Bob gags, runs away and comes back laughing.*

# Chapter 62

*Jean,*

*It's still Sunday about 7:30 p.m, I just made it home from a party. I am tired and sticky. The folds under my knees, my arms, elbows and toes, everything is so sticky, about to take a shower to cool down, unstick myself and then read for the rest of the night.*

*This month has gone by so fast, it's like I hardly left.*

*See you soon, take care.*

*Love Wayne*

# Chapter 63

*Monday, July, 1992*

*Hey, thinking of you.*

*It's all the way to Monday evening. I just put some brownies in the oven. I made tacos for dinner, I ate four, Big Mike ate five and Betty ate two. They were really good. I try to make dinner and do the dishes, just like in Denver. Today, not much happened.*

*Betty was not feeling that well. I would say that the 25 days that I've been here she has felt well for maybe four to five days and maybe felt okay another four days. Right now her stomach hurts. When she feels like this she takes a shot of Phenergan. I think, not sure. When she is awake she's very uncomfortable, she has trouble relaxing in her painful body.*

*I had a small talk with Ally and Tracy about Betty's spending and her money future. Betty buys a lot of things. It seems to flow everywhere, and they collect everything—plates, baseball cards, comics, stamps—you name it, and it is a limited edition of something, and they better get it, because if they don't get it now, they won't. It was a good talk. It's their thing, it's what they do, it's what we all do—we buy stuff. It gets Betty out of the house, they drive around, she sees things, they talk, spend time together and they have fun. Betty really enjoys herself when she goes out. She loves to buy whoever she is with everything.*

*Betty's health is rather unpredictable for her to volunteer anywhere. She may try a class at the rec center, maybe, she really loves what she is doing, spending time with the kids and grandkids, hanging with Big Mike. What would you rather do if you had a limited time to live? Do you want to learn to paint or hold Emma. Things are close to being right and good as they are.*

*Six months ago when I was here in January the amount of money that Betty had in her savings account is pretty much the same amount of money except for a bit she lent to Big Mike. So, she and the girls are pretty much spending what she gets from her social security and retirement. That's a good thing. We also talked about Betty's needs for the next year deductibles, bills, expenses. It was good to be on the same page, and no one was a jerk about anything, which we appreciate. The stuff that we did in January was huge, we couldn't be doing what we're doing without the benefits that are being reaped from January. We just need to be careful in case we miss anything that could come up and require attention. Betty needs to continue to do what she wants and spend the way she wants.*

*Tracy and Ally do so much in Dallas for Betty. They each have their own young kids that they are raising. Ally is a single mom with three kids under 10, she runs a daycare in her home. Tracy has five kids under 12. Way beyond what they do, lies what they feel. Feelings filled with incredible sadness at what is happening. Most of their life they live for each other and with each other. It is so strong, and for that to break, imagine the pain and the loss. Oh man.*

*I finished Book Two and started Book Three, good thing they're numbered. I read some stuff about interviews. Tomorrow I'm going to call and try to get an interview in Englewood.*

*Take care Jean, Love Wayne*

# Chapter 64

*Dear Jenny,*

*I'm pretty disappointed about Englewood High School. I didn't even get an interview. Shit. And there are a dozen things on top of that. For one, I'm sitting in Dallas reading fantasy novels. Fantasy. Sometimes it is. And then on top of that, when I get to Denver, I go camping in Aspen for a week. More fantasy.*

*I have to rethink my application, it doesn't compare to the competition. Others who are more qualified, have experience, get the interview. And there have only been a few job postings. There's not a lot of jobs, what's up with that? Few jobs while I read fantasy.*

*I have always thought that it would happen, and maybe it is happening, and I don't know what it is that is happening. I need to do more if I'm serious about getting a job. I've built up a casual attitude toward not working and getting a job, and this casualness is what*

*I put out there for the world to see!! Well shit. I'm going to finish this letter so the dismalness will end and I can go back to wondering about a bright future. I'm sure of that. You know why?*

*Love Wayne*

# Chapter 65

*Thursday, July 13th, 1992*

*Dear Jenny,*

*I'm sitting in the waiting room at Dr. Pounders office. Not too much is going on, it is a very hot day. Nick is here, he's 11, he's watching the people that come to see the doctor. I wonder what a kid sees or thinks about while sitting here, maybe it's just another doctor's office, everyone goes there.*

*How's it going in Denver? I'm looking forward to coming home. Now we're sitting in Pounders' office. Pounders will check up to see how Betty is doing and if her medication needs adjustment.*

*All is well according to the doctor, her blood is good and the CMV has not spread from her esophagus. Dr Pounders in January said Betty had 6-9-12 months, he based that on the CMV becoming active and spreading, which it is not doing. There will be longer. Treating AIDS you want to try and maintain where you're at. You don't really think in terms of things getting better, they don't. AIDS doesn't get better. You don't go to the doctors or the hospital to get better, there's no place to go to get better. You can't make it better. You don't live with AIDS. You die 'from' AIDS. Her death has become her life, it's become our life.*

*Hello, we are at CCC. Terry, a patient, just left, a medical coach picked him up to deliver him home. Terry was very thin, like what's ever on the other side of very thin, that's Terry. His eyes were sunken back into his head, his skin hugging his bones, a few strands of hair remain. Terry can't walk, not enough strength, not enough muscle mass to support his bones. He's in a wheelchair, nimble bony fingers clasped together twitching on a blanket that's covering hardly anything. He's on a respirator to breathe long faint breaths. No one is here to pick up Terry and what if no one is there when he gets home? Terry greatly moves*

*Betty. She sees what's there, what's coming. Toward the end it seems AIDS almost always comes the same way. She sees herself there, at some point you can't tell who's bones are in the wheelchair trying to breath. This image Betty has of herself terrifies her. Betty looks at Terry, she looks at me, and everyone looks the same, fear and pleading masking our faces. It is frightening, the possibilities are frightening.*

*Two lovers have just arrived driving a Jaguar, both good looking. One is HIV+ and they come together. It is a vow, for better and worse, sickness and in death, we shall be together. Would it bring you closer together? I guess it depends, it would certainly be a time to bail out. I mean golly, they aren't sure of transmission, and it's a death sentence. But if you do bail, what are you left with? You could say to yourself, "I left him when he needed me the most. I left when the pain got the worse." Or you could say, "I'm sorry, I'm scared, I don't want to die." One's about you, one's about him. Very hard choice. What if we dialed the choices back a bit. What if you are married and you said to yourself, "he needs me, we're married, it will get better." Or you could say, "I'm sorry but I want to go out, I want to live, enjoy things, do things, I am smothered here."*

*Everyone will choose differently.*

*I like the idea of going together to the edge, looking over to see the wonder all your hard work, all your life together brought you. You don't want to turn and leave, then you would never know what was beyond your dreams.*

*Where were we? At CCC. The CMV is there but not necessarily doing a lot of damage. What has happened, what is always happening and will continue to happen, is that Betty for the rest of her life will have these tormenting bouts with infections until the CMV begins to increasingly damage other organs and kill her. Doctor Pounders commented that she will certainly live through this Christmas and somewhere beyond. Anything beyond is mostly good.*

*We left CCC to go and buy some DDC. DDC is one of the two major drugs used to treat HIV, to fight the infections associated with AIDS. The other drug is AZT. The drugs used against HIV are called antiretrovirals. You take more than one drug. DDC was just approved by the FDA in June. Prior to approval Betty bought DDC from like a 'black market' had to pay cash, $60 for a month's supply. Now with FDA approval it looks like she will have to pay almost $500 for a month's supply from Eckert's. All of this, so much of the medicine and treatment for AIDS is new, they are still developing treatments, there is no precedent. It is happening right now. Why does it go from $60 to $500? Who can afford this? Wouldn't it be criminal if someone who needed it went without and they died because they didn't have enough money. Someone else has just arrived at CCC. A very thin man walked in, his belt wrapped twice around his body. His body is on the way to bones. He has a sort of pale gray* *face and very thin hair, one strand of hair covers a small part of his head. He walks in with his father, an old man, a very big man wearing cowboy boots, pants, shirts and cowboy hat. The father looks as if he has worked hard all his life outside. He's worked hard because you're supposed to. He prays to God each night. He is very thankful for everything he has, everything he has achieved he thanks the Lord for. He is a very grateful, good man. He believes God is there. Now he is here, is He? His son has AIDS. Why or how do you get dealt that? The father and son are here, they have come together, maybe that is more what this is about.*

*There is another poem, about a love between two people that feeds a third body; it is his son and that is all he knows. This third body that we feed with our love for each other, that's not a choice between two people. Robert Bly.*

*I've seen nine people today who are living with AIDS and dying. Each one of these nine are dying. Each one will be dead in this amount of time. Where else can you be like this?*

*The Thin Man stands up, his jeans were size 28 by 34, 28 inches and they were two times too big for all that is left of this man.*

*I guess my choices would be, first scenario, "I'm sorry, I'm leaving...", second one, "we're married, don't leave..."*

*What would you pick? Not sure if I'm still at that 70-80% normal. The choices may say something about you, but even if it does, it's who you are, a complete imperfect product I am.*

# Chapter 66

*Wednesday, July 14th, 1992*

*Dear Jean,*

*I'm at home now watching the All-Star game. Ted Williams threw out the first pitch. Tell Ryan that Wilson Phillips sang the National Anthem and see if she knows who they are? They were good.*

*Thursday*

*Time flies, it is some time Thursday afternoon. I hope it is not too much afternoon. At 2:00, I'm going to get a haircut and right now I'm sitting at Eckard's waiting for 6 prescriptions to be filled. At the doctor's, Betty and Pounders were joking that she is indeed the Antibiotic Woman, funny. Later in the day Betty said that it is all that keeps her alive, the drugs are all that keep her alive. I'm not so sure about it just being the drugs. People keep each other alive. All our lives we can bring life to others. We all keep her alive and she keeps us alive with her loving that finds its way out. That would be a good thing to try and do when I'm dying, put out all the love I've had for the people around me.*

*I was on the phone to a lawyer yesterday, first time for me and a lawyer, they're not as big as they seem. I do not know much, I'll learn as quickly as I can. They just called "Prescriptions for AntiBiotic Woman", gotta run, see you.*

*I had my hair cut today by a black girl from Houston Texas. She had just moved up to Dallas to get things going for herself. She liked to talk and she had a lot to talk about growing up black back in Houston. She had a story of being chased away, stories of hate.*

*I'm on my way this afternoon with Big Mike and Betty to see Catherine the Great exhibit at Fair Park. We've had tickets forever and have really looked forward to this. Read plenty of books and articles to get to know about Catherine. She became Great after killing her husband, Peter III. She became Empress of Russia for 34 years. That's a long time to be in power. Catherine put Russian culture, art, and thought out there to be recognized by Europe.*

*Betty's feeling okay, she's been in bed most of the day sleeping.*

*I was about to say that all I know about lawyers is what I've read or seen in the movie, so I don't know much. The lawyer yesterday was interested in our case and rather excited about two or three areas. He mentioned that there is one aspect of a potential case, that he would put his money on us. Didn't really describe what aspect, who knows what it all means, some of it is rather grandiose. I will find out a little more tomorrow and then we'll decide if it will be worth it to go through everything I've seen on tv dealing with the legal system. I tend to doubt we will go much farther, it's got to take tremendous effort and energy.*

*You need a guide that can help you through stuff, that explains how to deal with the associated stuff with professionals, insurance companies, employers, lawyers and the ones who demonstrate no regard. AIDS has to be regarded, seems close to an epidemic.*

# Chapter 67

*Thursday, July 15th, 1992*

*Dear Jenny*

*I haven't been in the back for a while and it is really nice this morning. There is just a wee bit of blue skies, see it, no sun in sight. A continual breeze gently blows, the trees bustle and the chimes whisper. The sound is in the silence. We have to stop, become silent and we'll hear it. We'll see it, a reflection of the morning heat rising. Everything is out there, available and we have a level of choice in how we are. Look, there goes a strand of happiness, attached to her heart. And there is a strand of bitterness attached to someone I may envy. I'm going to grab the strand of happiness and I'm going to go over here and say hello, good to see you, how you been and I'm going to listen to you. I'm going to create something good. I don't know, do whatever you do that is cool. Or I'm going to go to the park and complain about the path being wet and there are too many people. I'm going to create yuck. I'm not going to see people's enjoyment, or the flowers or the color of the sky. Sure won't hear any trees or chimes.*

*Just filled the bird feeder and bird bath. Betty scrubs the bath out for the birds to be clean. It's a nice overcast day.*

*Ryan sounded great last night on the phone, her voice was full of excitement about life changes. She has a spirit of growth as she heads out of childhood toward a teen angel. She sounds good, she's doing it with spirit, joy and confidence.*

*I'm bummed out about Ross Perot. I'm surprised and saddened by the polls. It is weird how the polls are affected. Clinton's story about him being one of us and how he's willing and able to save the American way of life and we should thank him. And then the things said by the other side can so damage Perot. Where we headed?*

*Well I have to go, my time cut short by the air conditioning man coming shortly to fix our three plus days of broken air conditioner, and time to get ready for the 10:00 a.m. appointment with David Someone, an attorney. I'm looking forward to coming home.*

*Love Wayne.*

# Chapter 68

*Saturday, July, 1992*

*Dear Jenny.*

*Seems like long ago since I wrote, now soon I'll be leaving here for Denver.*

*Betty and Big Mike are taking a nap. We just met Tracy and Ally at El Fenix for my birthday party. They gave me a Collector's Holiday Barbie for my birthday that they were saving for me! I was surprised. People at other tables were surprised, catching glimpses of me as I was unwrapping and they wondered about me. And according to them, now they know about me. I told Bob it was what I always wanted, he believed me. Everyone was drinking margaritas including Betty. It was a lot of fun, lots of laughing and real enjoyment, it was as if nothing else was going on except the wonderful moment of us all being together, being briefly flung out of the circle of pain.*

*It is with disbelief for most, that I'm leaving. Betty couldn't believe that I would be leaving. Big Mike was surprised, same with Ally and Tracy. We have become a part of each other's lives. Who we are, what we each bring, it will be missed. It is weird, the laws of attraction between brothers and sisters between mother and kids. I guess that's where it all started, as kids and that part remains. I will miss them, and there will be moments when we wish I was here.*

*Betty is or seems proud of me. It comes out during the last couple days while we have been shopping, at the lawyers and in front of other people. She is proud of who I am, proud that I am here and that I'm her son. And she loves my hat. She always wants me to wear my hat, she says it makes me look handsome, it's orange. Only a mother.*

*So glad to be here, it's got to be paradise.*

*Yesterday I went to Waco with Ally to drop her kids off at a McDonald's to meet Steve. The kids will stay with him for 3 weeks. He looked the same, older, and a bit square. I guess he is 44 and on his way to 50. That's how he dresses, like it, and how he is. Great.*

*After Waco we stopped at Tracy's. She too may even think something of me, and she is tough to please. She was sorry that I was leaving.*

*Ally and Tracy do a lot in Dallas with and for Betty. I mean a whole lot and this is on top of what they have to do in their own life, a life like everyone else's, most everyone, with the struggles, the fear, the hurt and heartache. So as much as I am, it's no wonder they like having me or anyone here. I felt sorry for Tracy last night when she was laughing, smiling and enjoying herself, even though you know it's there. Things can be hard here. Tracy and Ally seem so young.*

*I'm very grateful for this trip, it was fun and loving. I had a great time, so did Betty and everyone else. Although there was the absence of anything big done like in January, it's good. You don't always have to do stuff to maintain. It was a trip to relax and enjoy the time that we have together. I'm glad to be a part of this. The time is good and so will be the memories. Betty is living and dying right now at the same time and it's going to be okay. Take care, see you soon.*

*Love Wayne*

# Chapter 69

*Thursday October 8th, 1992*

*Dear Jenny*

*Golly, I'm in Dallas. How is it that that's how it is? It is crazy.*

*Good to talk to you. Sorry to hear how hard it is for you since you lost some clients, it weighs down upon things and causes projections. Stay away from projections, they may or may not happen or may happen differently. You're good at what you do, you have empathy and you seek understanding. It's all new. It's crazy, our jobs, working, actually not working. Not sure how things would fit together any other way though.*

*Betty and I went out shopping to the mall and sure enough it happened. There were things that I had to have, there were other things that if I didn't get now, I never would. It's pretty crazy but that's how things will work.*

233

# Chapter 70

*Tuesday, October 13th, 1992*

*Hello Jenny,*

*Right now we are at Dr. Pounder's office. It's Tuesday morning. The morning is going well with just a couple things that we have to do and then we should be home.*

*On our way in, an old mother with rugged skin that had been darkened by the sun was pushing her baby in a wheelchair. Hard to tell his age, 26 years old. The human body was never meant to be alive like this; his cheeks were caved in, his skin was pulled tight against his bones, his elbows were pushing out of his skin, his head was hanging in his lap, his whole body seemed to be working hard trying to curl itself into a fetal position, wanting to go back to where it came from. Betty's eyes fell gently on his soul and her body seemed to go numb, frozen for a moment, her eyes shuttered, blinked quickly to snap out of it and she couldn't, transfixed, and then intense fear washed over her. And forever Betty doesn't speak.*

*How would you f****** like that? Let me show you a picture of how your mother, how your baby, let me show you a picture of how they will look if they were HIV+. Or look at this picture, it's of yourself. You can have progression pictures, each month for the next 6 months, 12 months, all the way to the end. Look at the progression of you with HIV and tell me when you want to stop. Tell me when it's enough pain and you want to stop. Would you stay to see the last picture?*

*It's hard for me to believe that Betty will live that long, where her body has become so depleted. The son's spirit, soul seemed to have left his body, there wasn't enough left, it was a shell of bones. The loneliness, the pain, sadness, have driven away friends and happiness, driven away all he has experienced. It has driven away his spirit, and the boy's cries of pain can't be heard.*

*The lobby is crowded with people who are HIV+. One man has his arms wrapped tightly around his body so that nothing more can touch him or hurt him, his body crying out "please stop" he's so tired. What do you think would burst out if he burst? Sadness, fear, pain, loneliness. Three other people are here, a sister with her brother. The brother is with his partner or friend who is HIV+. The sister will not shut up, talking about her own s*** trying to calm herself while sitting here in this lobby with all of us around her. She doesn't want to stop talking, afraid that it will get her too. The brother and the patient have a hard time listening, it is so far from what is going on for them. But see there it is, why did I choose the strand about the talking girl? One guy sensing my fear, smiles as if to say that it will all be all right. Everyone here thinks I am HIV+, in their eyes, their reality, I do, I am. My mother is here with me and she is so wonderful and beautiful taking care of her son who she loves like no other. People think at the end it will be me who dies, not Betty.*

*How do you know when you think anything about anybody, you don't know the reality, you know your thoughts and that's your reality. We're all living in these different realities. But there is something else that has to mean more than this.*

*Betty is on her way out next stop CCC see you then.*

*Love Wayne.*

# **Chapter 71**

*Dear Jean,*

*We made it to CCC. As we were sitting waiting Betty talked about the old woman's son. She held my arm, she said she didn't want to live a life like the son. She said didn't want to be alive if she couldn't do things. Betty said she didn't want to be here if she felt we didn't want to be there. She didn't want the pain and suffering. She said she doesn't want to be alive when there is nothing left. She didn't want to lay there and waste away. And she said,*

*"You have to stop it, promise me"*

*"Please don't let this happen to me, promise me."*

*"Wayne, you have to promise me."*

# Chapter 72

*Wednesday, October 14th, 1992*

*It's later, it feels too late.*

*There's a point in time that Betty doesn't want to live.*

# **Chapter 73**

*Friday, October 16th, 1992*

*Hey Jenny,*

*It is Friday, late morning. How are you doing, glad it's Friday?*

*The other day the doctor said that Betty is doing well.*

*I remember last January that physically I thought Betty was as healthy as she would be. See I don't know.*

*It has been a pretty good trip.*

*I was thinking about my relationship with Betty and Tracy and Ally, what it was like 2 years ago. I didn't come up with much from back then, I like it now.*

*Every time I am here, the backyard becomes a sanctuary, the birds and squirrels, trees and bushes. It's a place where things around me play themselves out, in the backyard I can see things that happened yesterday and think about what may happen.*

*I need to finish this letter so I can mail it.*

*Betty has just awoken. She is on the phone to Tracy and they're talking about going Christmas shopping. Christmas in October, Betty is full of excitement. The idea is to shop early and then be able to shop later. Take care Jean, see you soon,*

*Love Wayne.*

# Chapter 74

*January-February 1993*

*Hello,*

*I lost pages. I lost the pages from the rest of the Dallas trip in October, 92 till now, February, 1993.*

*It looks like somewhere during that time Jenny and I have separated. Rats.*

*It picked up somewhere here....*

*We never knew where we were headed toward, look at us now, we hardly talk to each other about anything that matters to us, we don't talk about what we like or what we like to do, nothing about what we want? We're afraid of each other, afraid the other will bust you for something. We stay apart and now we both seem to be warmed by different fires.*

*Joey just barked and made me jump and that is why I*

*scribbled*

*Take care, Wayne*

# Chapter 75

*February 20, 1993*

*I don't know, I'm not sure how things will work out, I'm not sure where to even begin. Golly I wonder how many times in a life you begin over.*

*It's too cold to go outside. It always seems to be 11°, you go out and you're always wondering where your gloves and hat are and they're both on your head. I was walking Joey the other evening, the inside of my nose was freezing, and they say the same weather for the whole next week.*

*Right now all I do is hang out, I sweep a lot, still sleep, walk Joey and read. I read Truman's "At the FBI", started "At the Smithsonian" and I'm reading "The Creators" that Jenny gave to me for Christmas inside it says,*

*"Merry Christmas to you Wayne"*

*"I love you Jenny"*

# Chapter 76

*February, 1993*

*I guess there are different reasons for how we are together. There seems to have been love there, maybe it was not enough, or it was not real love. There's gotta be real love because regular love is not enough.*

*Emotions have different levels, you're a little sad, really really sad, devastated. Get a little mad, really really mad, you're out of your mind, psycho. You have a little love, really really love, paradise.*

*I also read National Geographic and school books. The reading part is not bad.*

*I also wait for the mailman to bring me something and for the phone to ring. Neither of those things ever happen and I'm waiting for nothing in particular anyway.*

*I also work out downstairs on a punching bag, I try to*

*hit and kick it as hard as I can.*

*So what may be wrong with walking the dog, reading, playing with the kids and working out? Not much except work and a job are important for survival and responsibility, and I could be doing both*

*The mailman just came, nothing.*

*Try not to forget Superman on the 21st or the 22nd, he dies, that's going to be a collector's edition.*

# Chapter 77

*Thursday, February 25th, 1993*

*Well there doesn't seem to be anybody to write to. Jenny and I are separated so I'm not going to sit and write her letters.*

*It has made me wonder, do you try and see how you got somewhere? Consider how you are? Or do you want to look at where you're going from here?  Seems we all have jobs, relationships, family, things that we do and who we are 'inside'. These things define our lives, who we are and they bring structure to our days. You wake up, eat, go to work, come home and eat, then we have 2-3 hours for relationships, families and the things that we do. We do have more time on the weekends, half that taken up by chores and the endless amount of housework that we do over and over, same thing, sweep, fold, put stuff away, it's crazy. According to this list that defines us and structures our day, I have no job, no relationship, and I have family every other week. What defines me, things I do and who I am, rats. The structure to your day is an adjustment. I don't have to do anything. How can that be, just went through the list and all I am and all I do is sweep. You need all these things in your life, job, relationships, all balanced.*

*With Jenny and I, I would say that there is something not there in our relationship. What is it that is not there? Commitment is not there. What does commitment come from? We could blame our parents for that. What you see and experience growing up. Not gonna blame them for anything. We're the sum of everything. Are there more separations and divorce by couples who grew up in separated families or in families that tried to stay together? Maybe there didn't even have to be a divorce, you grew up and you saw your parents disdain for each other, yet they stayed together and it seemed functional. You can try the same thing, cheat, lie, yell, talk sh*** about your* *spouse, it won't get you anymore than what you give. Don't you think? Like karma, what you put out there is what you're gonna get back. I believe that. Good and bad stuff. Even scientifically, you create a positive with a positive, negative with a negative, except for two negatives, that gets back to finding our comfort level when we are at odds with each other. I believe, if you do good things, say nice things then normally that's what will be around you.*

*There were things created in our relationship as a result of our life together. We say we love each other, and we want to love each other, is it enough to be happy with each other? No. I don't know, we are both tired, emotionally, and physically, and how far have we gotten, there seems to be more that we will go through and we would have been doing it with a fractured relationship. Maybe that's a progression, start with a small crack and then when it is up against anything out of the ordinary, cracks bigger. I don't know, There's something there, not much, maybe a little, maybe enough. There's also some relief or respite, our lives are hard together like they are right now, it could get worse for each of us like it is, so now maybe this is okay. Each emotion at its height creates another emotion.*

# Chapter 78

*Monday, March 1st, 1993*

*Still no one. And again.*

*I need to sit and talk about a list, a list to move me, somewhere, forward. Today was the day I stayed home and during my spurts of cleaning and aimlessness, I pretty much feel good about whatever is happening.*

*-look at refi the house right now I'm paying 10% interest, I could get it down lower, 7%, but who would refi me? I have no job.*

*-should commit to three contacts a week for a job. I have to get a job.*

*-need to write letters to Esterberg and Nesbitt.*

*-need to call Mary Ellen.*

# **Chapter 79**

*Tuesday, March 2nd, 1993*

*Hello, I know no one is there, so no more letter writing, it will be a journal now helping me find a way.*

*Overall things seem to be going pretty well. I don't have a job, but I do work and substitute. Jenny and I are separated. She's not here.*

*I have to find a place to go when I'm not here, I need a basement somewhere to live in. Jenny and I decided that Ryan and Tess would stay in the house and her and I would come back and forth every week. She'd be there a week and then she'd go somewhere and I'd be here a week and then I'd go somewhere, a basement. Now look, no job, a part time place to live. Ugh, don't like how this defines my life. We thought this arrangement would be a little easier, not as disruptive for the kids and they don't have to keep moving their stuff back and forth.*

*I think that with Jenny and I as long as it is going okay, let it go. It has to take some time to have a chance to see if the separation means anything. I need to be sure and not try to force anything, give it lots of space and time. If Jenny has made the decision to separate, it's not like she's going to change her mind in a week or two weeks or 3 weeks, who would do that? What would the point of it be? One or two or three weeks doesn't change anything, doesn't even get you to make a commitment to change anything in that amount of time. So I need to try really hard and not get all crazy and weird trying to put this back together. It's a separation so we'll be separate.*

*F****

*No job, no marriage, kids, AIDS, how do people do it? Remember the normal scale? 75% of the people will fall into the same scale I'm in, normal, like me. You can define normal however you want as long as it's normal, right? The other 25%, it's crazy, overwhelming, barely survivalable, way beyond what*

*I've experienced. The normal of us day-to-day are dealing with relationships, kids, jobs, illnesses, money. It's crazy. It's very hard, how do you do it?*

# **Chapter 80**



*Thursday, March 4th, 1993*

*Yesterday after subbing, I had a terrible headache, and then aggravated or intensified when Ryan and Tessa left. I didn't have a good day. School was nuts, kids were hard to get to do anything, toward the end of two classes, I was watching the clock to see how much more of this I would have to endure, it was hard, thank God I went back today? Learning is so far from these kids' minds, out of their minds. It took a lot of effort to get their attention and to keep it. You know what's crazy, students are allowed to smoke on campus in an area called The Commons. One kid who skipped school was out at The Commons all day. There was another student yesterday who did the same thing. They hang out, like at the mall, they just hang in The Commons instead of the mall because they know no one will bother them at school. The kids do what they want and no one bothers them. It's crazy. Puppy no, whoops*

*It doesn't sound too good for Betty. She is having trouble walking any distance. Her energy for walking is gone after a very short distance. It sounds like they may get a wheelchair, where does a wheelchair lead to? It is hard to be of distance, not being there.*

*I like sitting here, the lights are low, it is quiet except for the music that makes my feet dance on the floor. It's Van Morrison Hard Nose the Highway, "it may not be today, it may be tomorrow." It's not so bad. I miss the kids. They have a child's vitality and personality that is honest and in line with their whole being, whatever they're feeling or thinking is how they are.*

*I hesitated to go to dinner, different things made me hesitate, none of them too important, so I went. Neither of us, or both of us are the same as we were. We're each taking a different direction.*

# Chapter 81

*Saturday*

*Pretty nice morning. Mostly laid around and read five chapters in a Roosevelt mystery, good coffee, it was very nice.*

*Tracy called and said that Betty was doing just okay. I called Big Mike and he said that yesterday her temperature was always at 101°. If it had been 101 this morning, he would have taken Betty to the hospital. Mike was sincere, his voice was shaking with concern. For who? He said that Betty would lay on the couch and two blankets would not warm her, she would shiver and shake. The coldness came from inside her body, permeating everything. Betty couldn't eat, no snack, no taste, nothing.*

# **Chapter 82**

*A Tuesday in April, 1993*

*Most likely I should have worked. The choices were terrible, teach Spanish at a middle school or a late call came from another middle school. I was hoping for something better, it never came. It does.*

*It is hard to focus on Jenny and I. When I do they are thoughts of what led to the separation. We weren't connected, only by disagreements. There were resentments, I wonder if I've hardly ever compromised. Golly, what if I haven't. What if I thought I knew better? That's tricky. What do you do if you think you know better? You can present any argument and tilt to where it looks good on you, and I don't want to do that. Jerk.*

*I'm responsible for a lot of the transgression in our marriage. I'm not gonna spell out the first reason. The 2nd reason would be that maybe, possibly living with me, supporting me, loving me, takes a lot of energy, loss of identity, maybe loss of purpose as it becomes what my purpose is. Shit.*

*Maybe I sucked the life out of each of us. Maybe I sucked the life out of Jenny to where she no longer felt she was in control, or that she decided things, her thoughts not counting, she was not able to lead her life. I did. She felt like she had to follow. Same thing now again.*

*How normal is that? Dippin in the 60% of people who are like that, and there are different degrees and different reasons for that. It's not like I'm a total jerk. Shit*

*The third reason would be like I just wrote, I think I know better, and it is my way almost always. And that creates bad stuff between people, resentment, anger. When this stuff shows up, look what is moved out; fuller experiences, funner, kindness, love, compassion, empathy, all cast aside into the darkness of anger, despair, hate. Oh man this is terrible. I never changed much.*

*S***.*

*Fuller and Funner, you can name kids that.*

*When you feel it, you will know you are there, it will roll softly across you and then fade, don't let it fade fast.*

# Chapter 83

*Wednesday April, 1993*

*I saw Jenny this afternoon after school. I wish I could kiss her. There are an assortment of thoughts and emotions that bump up against each other and cause chaos. That's scientifically. Jenny looked pretty, nice, complacent, she was rolling along, like separation agrees with her. But we don't really know, right? Gotta be a drag. Funny. Later from something Jenny said, and once when I looked over at her, I felt a permanentness to our separation and felt a sadness about that, trepidation, mostly sadness. I looked at Jenny and saw something I hadn't seen before, I felt a loss.*

*What if we each walked around and each time our actions didn't follow our thoughts we'd get a little pipp. The pipp would make our elbow jolt out. It's probably better not to be twitching, or walk around holding your elbow. Seems some places… nevermind.*

# Chapter 84

*Evening*

*I saw Jenny again this evening, when the initial excitement and dreamingnes subsides, you can see, hear, feel, where we really are. Jenny seems distant from feelings about us, like she doesn't have any. Part of separating, and you know what? There slowly is no 'us', it disappears. Oh no. I did feel loneliness and sadness this afternoon. I missed Jenny and our relationship and our marriage, but what I miss, our relationship missed. There hasn't been a closeness for this long.....You have to go to the 80's, to find passion, you know how long ago the 80's were, all but forgotten. You have to have this stuff in a marriage, at least once in a while, not since the 80's. Fuck that.*

*I don't know*

# Chapter 85

*Sunday, March 13th, 1993*

*Well, I wasn't going to write for a while. I thought I was getting into a cycle of thoughts, so I didn't. It is now all the way to Sunday night. The days and nights seem like a continual drag. I remember Friday night feeling hurt and sad that some things are going to only be found in the past. These things have no present, and doubtful you find them in the future. You're moved in a direction you may not want.*

*"What if I don't want it to be like that?"*

*"Too bad. You have no choice."*

*"What? How can I have no choice in something I'm a part of?*

*"What you're a part of doesn't exist anymore. What you were a part of is something else now, and you're not a part of it."*

*That's crazy, it sucks. I've been a part of that for almost half of my life, now look, to slow, it's f***** gone. It's like why aren't there things that mean more, our relationship and myself not meaning more. Hurt and sadness often travel together. And then when you're traveling this road, you find yourself alone. I'm not quite used to being alone, no kids around, no Jean around. I remember that these feelings sort of hung out there awhile.*

*And I don't see a lot of people with any such better relationship that we're capable of having. I was talking to Katie. She was surprised and thinking about her own tolerance. We all know what we want in our relationships, more involved, lighter, room for error and don't forget fuller and funner. We're all human, all living, all make mistakes and sometimes there is no room for mistakes, that is impossible.*

*Do Jenny and I comfort each other? Sometimes. Is our relationship best for each of us? Almost could be.*

# Chapter 86

*Tuesday March 16th 1993*

*It's evening, talked to Jenny and made some plans with Katie tomorrow at St Patrick's Day. I can't really tell how, why or when the relationship with Jenny deteriorated, it's like it's so gradual how slowly it swallows a marriage. You can hardly notice it, it becomes more of your life, more of your regular life, becomes your way of life, gradually the hugs, holding, kissing becomes less frequent till none. Remember how you kissed your wife when you first met? Remember the passion you felt? It was like my God this is it, paradise, I found it. What would you give for that again?*

*The changes are subtle. You start to roll with them and it gets late, then too late. Look at this example. I said to Jenny to stop demonstratively reading all the commas while she was proofreading something I had written, I use a lot of commas. She responded by not wanting to read at all, putting it down and leaving. It was a set up by one of us. We were talking at dinner and neither one of us knew what the other was saying and it was still quarrelsome. We are fighting about different things while fighting with each other. Nobody wants to change. We have miles to go before we meet again. Jenny and I seem selfish. What she wants to do involves no compromise. Funny I should use that word. I was sort of disappointed and yet it made me feel okay about what we're doing with the separation. Our relationship was once upon a time, built upon love, compassion, caring, support. Once was and it hasn't been. Recently it seems being built with small blocks of what we say or do each day. These blocks of bickering are replacing the foundation of our relationship. The little things that happen every day, saying things to each other, telling each other something, getting mad at each other, all these blocks could have almost bounced off the love, they may impact but not define us. These are the things that have come to matter to both of us. These things are replacing once upon a time.*

*It's hard to explain things.*

*Neither of us are the culprit or to blame, both of us are responsible.*

*What we're doing is who or how we have become.*

# Chapter 87

*St. Patrick's Day*

*March 17th, 1993*

*Wednesdays are always sad days when the girls leave.*

*How do you preserve their beauty, their youth and wonder?*

*Jenny and I are fading.*

*I don't seem to be doing anything about it.*

*Each time one of us says something the other wants to leave and go outside to wait. We are something else now.*

*It is almost 100% impossible for us to talk about anything.*

*We definitely saw enough of each other this week.*

*If I could change to whatever I want, I would want to be married.*

*Not like it is now, we can't be together right now.*

# **Chapter 88**


*Monday, March 21st, 1993*

*Still writing to no one. Well not really no one.*

*I need to step it up. A feeling of despair has lingered over me. Part of it, big part, is money, can't even pay $300 for a brake job, I'm broke. I guess this figures if you're not working, you're gonna get broke. No money is a drag and having nowhere to get it is a bigger drag. I need to do two or three things, or 10 things. I need to try and patch money things together and hope I make it till... when? I need to make it till August, 6 months, half a year I just need to make it till then, and then what? August starts a new school year so I'll have a job and a paycheck, benefits, insurance, vacations, I will have it all. And in August it will be 6 months out with Jenny and I. By then we will both know what we want to do. We will both know if we try to get back together. If we don't, it seems we should by then be*

*able to handle whatever it is that is going on between
us. Do you think? That'd be 8 months of living apart,
separated, it seems you will have adjusted and able to
carry on. Right? 75%?*

# Chapter 89

*Tuesday morning, March 23rd 1993*

*One of these days is my bygone anniversary.*

*I did work this afternoon. I have felt really bothered this morning. I don't know why. The car is still at the shop hanging over my head like a sword. I guess I was hoping Jenny would have said something to her mother and then she would have helped us out. There is no 'us' though. You gotta adjust a lot in your head, whatever was there before is gone, same with what was in your heart, it's gone. Period. Don't rush the refill though.*

*I always tell Harry and everyone I'm doing okay and I'm not doing as well. Most people probably do the same, "oh, I'm good." It's hard for people to always know what they need, even harder to ask for it. Things are not good. If I added up the things going on with me, I'd get 0. That's terrible. Maybe I'd get a couple points for who I am. Shit, I'm a 2, that's funny. Seems like everyone I know is more than that, crazy, in that case if anyone asks I'll say 3, no 7. Or I'll change the criteria, get rid of having a job, a marriage, a home, money, someone to hold. If I take those things off the scale... what's left to measure? Mostly you. Then what would you be?*

*Top is coming and going and I still have different anxieties about that. I am a little fearful, it mellows out the rough edges, it shows a different light upon situations and makes things look a little easier. I sit there, take it all in and blow it all out.*

*Sometimes I'm not sure what to do or when to do it and it has made me so complacent, I didn't move sometimes when I should have. One day at a time I have to get things done and not mess with other things. I'm thinking I'm losing some of the 70%, those who would be doing a lot more than I.*

*It's a little later in the afternoon. I worked, working*

*helps, too much idleness. I need to work everyday for the next 3 months.*

*Induced from the top, I felt a strong surge leave my body, it's hard to explain. It's like starting to separate from things, letting things break away. When this happens you don't feel the burden of these things. I don't know. Some things I want to be away from sometimes.*

*Things I write are only thoughts, not real in the sense they manifest, although they might, but real in the sense they are thoughts, and they are in your head. They lend themselves toward reality. Your thoughts, their interpretation, their manifestation are your reality. All these realities we live in, it's crazy, thank God we are distracted by jobs, people, the stuff we do all day, these distractions keep reality at bay.*

*I've had many thoughts and emotions about separation, jobs. The kind of emotions that chase you into a corner. Sadness and despair, sadness and fear, sadness and anger, sadness and relief. They all start with sadness. I wonder if that is the persuasive state of my being, sadness.*

*I feel like I have to do a lot, but I don't know which direction to go.*

*I need to get a job. But the thing too is that having a job will interfere with what I want to do with Betty.*

*In a way this all works.*

*I want to be outdoors more, hiking, fishing, camping.*

*I want to be away so I can find my own way.*

*I want to be with Betty. I'm pretty much ready to go to Dallas.*

*I haven't mentioned the kids because it would sound corny. I've left Jenny off of my list of wants or needs because it isn't time to do anything about Jenny or the marriage. When you get separated you have to be separated, it has to be allowed to happen, if you try to*

*unseparate it, it becomes more separated. Separation
has to be able to happen.*

# Chapter 90

*March, 1996*

*Dear Wayne,*

*I guess you've been gone for about an hour. I can tell I'm not going to handle this well. I'm glad it's a rainy day, because it fits my mood. Thank you for the bracelet, it means a lot to me. God, I want to be with you. Just thinking about holding you makes my stomach go crazy. I know I was attracted to you this summer but I never expected to feel this intense about you. I don't think you're here to save me, I know only I can do that. I just want to have a love affair with you. I want to be able to hug you in a room full of people and I want to lie in your bed with you. I remember the first time I kissed you, I closed my eyes and felt the softness of your lips, it was right after ice cream. Do you know what I dream about? It's late, I better go, meeting in the morning.*

*Good night, I love you.*

*Julie*

# Chapter 91

*Friday, March 26th, 1993*

*Betty is in Baylor Hospital. It's hard to focus or consider much else besides Betty.*

*I spoke with Betty on the phone, she sounded small and so quiet. Where do you go inside yourself when you are dying, or if you are really hurting, where is there comfort?*

*The hardest part for Betty is that each time she is sick, she thinks it is the beginning of the end of her life. Wouldn't that be out of this world? You have a disease that is going to kill you and each time you get sick, you think this is the time. The time of your death has arrived. Then it's delayed, comes again and again.*

*She talked about dying and not living anymore. There is intense physical pain, there is even more emotional pain, she can hardly bear these episodes anymore.*

*I don't think we are at the end.*

*I feel bad, so tight, I wish I was on top. You know how it is when it is all around you, circling, and it won't go away, it's howling for you. I don't know. I'm not sure what to do now. I don't know what to say, I feel like I can't move, nothing seems familiar to me. I don't recognize this stuff around me.*

*Tracy said Betty lost 10 lb in 2 weeks. She hasn't left the house for 2 weeks. She is dehydrated, her stomach is not functioning correctly, her bowels are not functioning correctly, things aren't correct at all. I picture Betty lying in bed, her face as beautiful as ever. There is red around her cheeks, her eyes are closed, she is sleeping and she doesn't want to wake up.*

*It's later in the night. I talked to Betty, Tracy, Linda, Harry and Jeff.*

*I started crying while I was talking to Betty, she sounded so young and precious. I thought I was talking to someone much younger, her voice was so soft and quiet, peaceful. Betty said she was very tired, 4 hours of tests and they are still looking for something. They are emptying her stomach through her nose. They inserted a tube through her nose into her stomach and it sucks out whatever is in there. It's very uncomfortable. Picture this and tell me how it happens like this?*

*Betty told me she loved me. My heart exploded.*

*"Wayne, I love you."*

# Chapter 92

*Tracy called and told me an incredible story about Harry. Harry brought a priest to the hospital to see Betty. Really heavy stuff, out of this world stuff, and it was all natural for Betty to talk to a priest and God. They spoke alone. Last Rites? Last Rites are to release you from pain and suffering.*

*After they talked, Ally, Tracy and Harry came back into the room. Harry was to the side of the room and he was crying. Ally was crying and Betty was crying. Tracy said Betty was sad and scared, she felt it getting so close to her. Little doubt about what is coming, it is all right there. Tracy said that Betty was very relieved to talk to the priest and glad that the priest had come. I bet it was like heaven. I called Harry and told him what a wonderful thing he had done. It was sad talking to Harry about this, he was so compassionate, so in love. This far removed from one another, and there is something very strong there. Like what could it be?*

*Maybe it's the lock box in love. The small golden locks that look like hearts made of gold. There is a key and if you open your heart you'll find your true love.*

*It was all very sad and full of beauty and love. What Harry did meant a lot to Betty and Betty meant so much more to Harry. It's a wonderful, wonderful thing.*

# Chapter 93

*Saturday, April 3, 1993*

*I'm in Dallas.*

*3 Non Blondes are singing loudly "What's Going On" on Big Mike's big stereo. I hear this song again later and it was blasting again, I was wondering what the f*** was going on, I had just dropped off Big Mike at Love Field for him to go see his mom. I was sort of out of my mind then. The song is banging out thoughts that bang around in my head. It's nice like this.*

*The morning is cold, my feet are cold and I have a cold, bad one. I feel hungover. It has been arousing 24 hours. This time yesterday I was smudged in a tiny seat on Sun Country. I was sitting next to Bill Owens, a long hair singer in a country western band that just won a competition in Colorado, he said. Bill is going home now to his apartment and 8-year-old daughter. He just declared Chapter 13 Bankruptcy. He makes* *about $21,000 a year and likes to hunt Civil War buttons/bullets in Virginia. Crazy. Who do you think is better off the country western singer or the preacher?*

# **Chapter 94**

*Later in the afternoon*

*I went to the hospital, Betty was awake and lucid. We were able to sit for a while and talk. The topics and stories flowed one to another. Betty almost started to cry while she was talking about Jenny and I. She was upset, sad, she was concerned about me and concerned about me being married or separated. She doesn't want anything to happen to me that would hurt, it all seems to hurt.*

*We talked about Betty growing up and she told more stories when she was young with her sister, Barbara and her mother. Betty seemed to love the time when she was young, it sounded so freeing, there were no confines to how she lived, there was no fear of anything bad happening, it was as if she could run and jump through the air wherever they went. She spoke about being young and then growing up she began to see the hardness appear and the richness and innocence being zapped away from us by the fearful and the selfish.*

*Betty can't remember one bad day when we were kids, instead it was all happy stories about what we did and where we traveled to. Betty loved our trips to Rome. Harry taking us into places we shouldn't have been, farther into the Catacombs, up into St Peters. We were in the Westport news because when we went to Rome it was before the traveling had really started. Harry in his job with United, Braniff and Pan Am, started a lot of these routes and we were the first ones there. Betty loved the trip to Hawaii. Hawaiians greeting us in grass skirts, placing flower leis over our heads. It was real stuff. It was like we discovered Hawaii. The trip to Hong Kong, seeing our food alive before we ate it at the big floating restaurant. Betty loved everything, she loved most of her life. She mentioned something about being in love and I said I didn't know.*

*Now I'm sitting here in a daze, resting while all of*

*these black birds are feeding in the backyard. You know what, if I could talk to someone right now I would want it to be Jenny. I miss her sometimes dearly, there is an emptiness, there's a desire to share with her.*

# Chapter 95

*Sunday, April 4th, 1993*

*Today I woke up early, showered, ironed and went to Tracy's. I was there for a moment and then off to the hospital, this time with Dan. This will be my fourth attempt with the third person in the last 48 hours to get the Mercedes started. To everyone's surprise, including Dan's, I think, except for Tracy, he got the car started. Amazing.*

*We had a nice visit with Betty. She was a lot better in some ways. She is better when she's in the hospital, the level of care is higher, so it's good in a way she's here.*

*From the hospital I went to Tracy's. She was on her way to the grocery store, I went with her, we shopped, went back to the house for 7 minutes and off we went to the car mechanic! We did that in Richardson and with about a minute to spare off we went to Nic's preseason baseball game. We left halfway through and went to Betty's, no one was there, we hung out for a while and then while saying goodbye to Tracy, Big Mike and Betty arrived home from the hospital. I don't get it.*

# Chapter 96

*Monday, April 5th, 1993*

*Our first day home started exactly 2 hours ago when I was startled from my sleep by Catherine, a young, big home care nurse. At one point I had to ask Catherine to back way off from her "specific procedures" that she said she had to follow to the T.*

*Fuck the T. And then after an incredibly long hard time with Betty, underneath my breath I thanked Catherine for her patience, concern and professionalism that she practiced to the T.*

*When Catherine arrived Betty had been startled from her induced sleep. And then she was just nuts, it was all nuts, it was so crazy, out of mind stuff. For almost the whole morning Betty would hobble back and forth down the hallway to the den and back to her bedroom, back and forth, and I followed her as she tried to find a way to settle herself down. She couldn't find comfort in anything there was, if she could have ran she would have, she wanted to get away, she was frantic. I'm not sure why, I don't know if it was the drugs, her condition, I don't know, it was just freaking crazy. And finally, after forever, Catherine began to see how far out this was, she got it, and so gently and with pure love and comfort, Catherine said "Betty, Betty please lay down and rest, it will be okay."*

*And Betty laid down and she cried. And I died. It was so unreal, it was the most alive time to die.*

*It's later. Catherine has left. Betty's slowly leaving. When I look out I don't see anything except a white wall that stops everything.*

*All during the time with Catherine the phone was ringing. It was crazy, there was a non- stop ringing, I could hear it everywhere. It would be the dentist wanting to know if Betty was going to make it to her appointment. Tracy called. A nurse called, Pounders called and someone called about the Mercedes. Big*

*Mike called twice about something that was so far away, our realities on different planets. The ringing was loud, nothing would stop.*

*Betty hasn't been able to eat much, she drank some juice, a bite of an English muffin and three bites of French toast. Now she has had a shot of something that has shut everything down and she is gently swaying in her mind, in her own world. What's it like between shots?*

*There are finches that have come to Betty's bird house. The finches are just beginning to make it their home, still checking it out, they haven't started to move in yet. The new feeder does not get as much activity as the big old bird feeder stuck in the mud.*

*Here's a list of things I'm going to do tomorrow:*

*-call about an airline ticket*

*-call insurance lady about benefits*

*-call about meals being delivered by St. Rita's*

*-call Presbyterian insurance*

*-call Resource Center about Nelson Tebedo insurance payment*

*-eye medicine ?*

*-Betty's bills*

*-handicap parking*

*-Father Vogel for prayers*

# Chapter 97

*Monday, April 5, 1993*

*Hello,*

*It happened again. That's what it is going to do, things are going to happen over again. There will be no time when things are over, this is only the beginning of things. Each time you're affected, there will be more. It will only stop at the end.*

*I bet it doesn't ever reach any imaginable limit. The pain and the suffering could be endless.*

*I went into Betty's room, I thought she would be in bed. She was on the bathroom floor, trying to throw up, gagging, spitting up bile. She was lying on the bathroom floor lost, muttering about life, muttering senselessly, muttering about how sick she was, crying for it to stop. I sat on the floor next to Betty.*

*I stayed as close as I could get, I wasn't going to leave*

*the bathroom floor and I didn't want her to leave. I was quietly crying, inside I was screaming.*

*We stayed on the bathroom floor forever and when it was quiet and peaceful. I got her up, cleaned her up and moved her into the bedroom and there she sat naked on the side of the bed, her head hanging down gently moving back and forth. I sat next to her and gently scratched her back. It was out of this world. I felt like I was sitting there with a big, old angel. An angel ready to hang up her wings. I was comforting an angel. Betty whispers that she's dying, she said she doesn't know what to do, she has to let herself die, she said it's hard to hold on.*

*I wrapped my arms around her and held her. I don't know if I was breathing, I didn't have to. I wasn't thinking, my body was there, my heart was pounding, my mind was lost.*

*Betty laid down and closed her eyes as if she would fall into a deep peaceful sleep.*

*I left, the phone rings, it's Tracy. It's hard to tell Tracy about Betty, they're connected and I couldn't breathe, my chest was heaving trying to take a breathe and I could hear Tracy saying "Wayne, Wayne, tell me what's wrong." I couldn't. I got off the phone, went back into Betty's room and there she was naked, sitting up in bed, her arms frantically searching for something that's not there. Bile, something, was running down out the side of her mouth and she was crying. She started to cry more when she saw me come in. She doesn't want to be seen like this. She started trying to thrust needles of Demerol into her port. She doesn't know what she is doing, trying to stop the pain.*

*You know how f***** crazy Demerol is? It's used for severe pain. It's like your pain level is over 100 and the Demerol will bring it down to 20. I don't know if I know what is causing the pain, I don't know if they know, but that's not what is being treated, Demerol treats the pain intensity through your brain, it somehow alters your mind in terms of how you feel* *pain.*

*I stopped in the doorway for a moment, it seemed like a surge of pain, fear and hopelessness ripped at my body, but I couldn't feel anything. The hopelessness didn't really overwhelm, there was more a sense of gentleness, understanding, love. I went over to Betty, took her in my arms and held her forever.*

*Here I am now, sitting, sipping coffee in the sun feeling as if I had fallen a thousand feet, crashed and didn't feel a thing.*

# Chapter 98

*Tuesday, April 6th, 1993*

*The next 30 minutes I will be at CCC waiting for Dale to return. The only reason I'm here is because I had no place to go after going to Dr Pounders office, he was at lunch, so I thought I would try here. All of this after spending 45 minutes at Baylor Hospital waiting for the nurses who are trying to find Betty's pillow! She wants her pillow. I have it now.*

*I thought today I would get out, get something done, learn something.*

*I want to find out more about Betty's health. I don't know. I'm not clear what exactly it is I want to know, it seems like there's gotta be something to know. Like where is Betty at? Is there a chart? How can it get worse? Is she at any stage? What about the drugs? The drugs are crazy. Does knowing anything help anything? But then it's like if I told you what was coming, what would you do? Prepare yourself? Like would I have been prepared to find Betty lying in her vomit on the bathroom floor? Or prepared when Betty is sobbing that she can't go on. I don't know, you pick.*

*There is a lot of variance with HIV, how it affects each of us. Because of Betty's age and sex, they don't know, she's one of the few females. You will know when it happens.*

*My car didn't start after CCC, jumped it and went back to Dr. Pounder's office. That was a mistake because when I was done there, the car didn't start. An old couple stopped to help, couldn't, an old man tried to jump start the car, couldn't. I was f*****. And this was after picking up the car 3 hours ago with a $300 new starter guaranteed, my ass.*

*Then an old black garage attendant bet me $15 he could start the car. I raised the bet to $20. He came out with big fat jumper cables, and his rebuilt 20 ton pickup truck, the Mercedes roared to a start, gave him* *his $20, and as he backed up, all 20 tons rolled into the front of the Mercedes and broke the grill.*

*It's 5:00 p.m. Betty is feeling better today. So crazy from yesterday. Yesterday was shocking, out of this world and now she's back.*

*I did talk to Dale today. He gave me a big comforting hug, he knows where we were yesterday, he's been there, knows there are no words that can lend comfort.*

*Dale talked about AIDS. He said that Betty would not be able to eat, her stomach shuts down. It is not something they fully understand medically. Something happens, he used the word 'wasting'. There's not a lot anyone can do. The person just can't eat, nothing feels good or feels right. They start to lose weight, lose muscle. They start to waste away. Betty will waste away. Now I see. The patients in the wheelchairs don't have the muscle to walk, their heads in their laps, they don't have the muscle, the skin wrapped around bones, it was wasted away.*

*Dale said that AIDS patients can live like this for 3-6 months, they can live without eating, they use TPN and with nothing else. TPN isn't like a feeding tube that goes into your stomach. TPN will go through Betty's port directly into her blood and it will supply Betty with the vitamins and nutrition that she needs to stay alive. TPN will be the only source of nutrition for Betty. TPN doesn't stop the wasting, it keeps you alive while you turn to waste. Betty will waste away.*

*F*** that, did you hear me, I'm screaming F*** that.*

*This can't happen.*

*Dale said that this is the beginning of things beginning to happen. So like a new beginning. All the very important things that we were all doing, they are no longer important, there's now all this unbelievable new stuff that it's important.*

*Dale said that there wasn't going to be very much we can do during this time. There will be no treatment until a symptom or an infection arises, then they can treat the infection. It's almost as if there's a big gaping hole in the treatment plan. We will fill the hole with comfort, touch her, hold her each time.*

*This is how it is going to happen, how it always happens.*

*Dale is an angel sent down by God to explain to people and give comfort.*

# Chapter 99



*Wednesday, April 7th, 1993*

*Betty is laying in bed, sleeping, I think induced. Her condition has slightly improved since Monday. Improved meaning that last night she spoke about five sentences about an old LVN who worked on her floor. The old LVN hadn't kept up and didn't know how to do enough and everyone would help her and do her work and her charts. Betty said she felt so sorry for this old LVN because the LVN had worked with cancer up until the day that she died. And no one ever knew. Betty said that she was so thankful that she had quit work, had left and has time before she dies. This sounds odd and fortunate. It's odd that Betty considers this 'time' before she dies. I'm not there, I hope for more. Working consumes most of our time, most of our energy, and I hope time after working is more than this. The fortunate part is much better, Betty thinks, she believes that she has time to be thankful for. I don't know.*

*This is about all Betty has done during the past three days. She doesn't eat, can't walk, can't take baths, can't read. She lies in bed and sweats and tries to endure the pain.*

*I think each of us hopes for one more time when she will rise out of bed, get dressed, she comes out into the den, and smiles at each of us. She looks beautiful and says, "I'm ok"*

# **Chapter 100**

*Wednesday, April 7, 1993*

*It is only 12:10 p.m. it feels like it has been all day forever.*

*Two nurses, Sue and Donna, have been here for the last 3 hours. They were here to clean and change Betty's port, and they found her in pain. The pain continued and the whole scene was too much for Betty, she vomited all over herself while the nurses were working on the port. They flinched. Then a thin spout of blood came out the port. They freaked. You could see it, you could hear it, you could feel it everywhere, the fear and horror as this disease is being spread over Betty and them. The nurses were frantic, calling out to cover themselves, to try and shield themselves.*

*"There's blood coming out, grab that pad!"*

*"Quick cover that please"*

*"Oh my God."*

*"Look at my glove, I need a new pair of gloves quickly."*

*"Please hold this, don't let it go."*

*"Watch out for that, be careful."*

*All around this is happening, and Betty is crying, crying because no one wants to touch her, no one wants to be near her, no one wants to be here.*

*No one wants to touch Betty. No one wants to touch you.*

*She was in so much pain. She couldn't move, she couldn't sit up, she could hardly lift her head and when she did her eyes would search wildly for something to help her, something to stop the pain, searching for a way out. Her eyes would race from nurse to nurse and settle on me, piercing my eyes, crying for help. She was frantic, holding on for dear life, she could not stop searching, her eyes pleading, pleading for something to be done. Please don't do this to me. It seemed like her whole body and mind were losing it. She wants it to stop.*

*Time stopped and meant nothing. I have never in all my life seen someone in so much pain and suffering. In all my life added together, never so much, way way beyond.*

*Everything was there in the room, constantly it was right in front of you and there was not a moment to think of anything before the next thing was happening. There were no thoughts, actions moved by emotions. It was so rapid. All of it going inside of you, not a moment for it to come out, the next moment blacks out everything else. What will happen when there is a moment? And everything explodes from inside of you?*

*Have you ever seen fear in someone's eyes, have you ever heard fear in your own voice? I think what just happened was way beyond what we were built for.*

*Way beyond how we live, beyond how we are trained,
beyond what we know about ourselves. Everything
was exceeded.*

*The pain, the hurt, the fear, the anger all wrap
themselves tighter and tighter into a deadly ball that
starts pushing from the inside. It's strange, you want
to scream and yell, you want to run, you want to be the
wild bull smashing everything.*

*The images are pressing themselves forever in your
mind.*

*Time passed while Betty was resting. The nurses and I
met on the back porch.*

*The nurses were upset, they were scared, they were
affected by what just happened and they didn't know
what to say. They didn't want to be here, they couldn't
believe what just happened. It was hard for them to say
what they were thinking, they wanted me to say it. They
wanted me to say how terrible it was and they wanted*

*me to decide what to do next. They wanted to know if we are done and want to move to a higher level of care, that it was ok for Betty to be put somewhere, left there, to die medicated, "it would be painless." They wanted to hear that we were ready. They wanted these decisions made. In their minds there was only one decision. They wanted something done now, call an ambulance and move her. It was on the other side of crazy and fear and pain.*

*I told them that we were not moving Betty. We're not ready. It's too early for that level of care. We have not prepared ourselves or Betty for this. We had to wait. We want Betty to be well again before we do anything. I told them that Betty didn't want to go to a nursing home or a hospital. She wants to be here in her house, she wants to die here, she wants to be surrounded by us. There's not going to be a nursing home.*

*The nurses were very reluctant to accept any type of waiting. They started to confront me about our ability to take care of Betty. They described what it was going to be like, they kept saying we had no idea what we're going to be up against. They said we had no idea what we're doing and that we could do more harm than good. They wanted to know how we were going to clean up after her vomit, how are we going to clean blood around her port, "What do you think you're going to do?" They were shocking with their horror stories. It started banging in my head and I had no place to go. I shut them off and could no longer listen or hear what they were saying. They finished. We said Betty was going to stay where she was and we'll find a way.*

*Now it is almost 6:00 p.m., the nurses have left and I can't move, I can't think.*

*I've been here letting this day sit in my head. I've lost feelings. I'm supposed to wake up Betty and do a blood sugar test. I take a little needle, prick Betty in the finger and prick her in the leg. I'm not going to.*

*It's like people are wired for so much. If you compare*

*us back to the man during the Paleomezoic Era, they had more strength, they had more instinct, they had more courage. That's what they needed to survive and we have evolved to where we don't need that stuff. Our development has taken us to a point where we experience and are able to handle certain levels of fear and courage. I think we each have experienced situations that smash up against what we can handle and how we have developed.*

*And some experiences are way beyond that. Way beyond what we were ever made to do. It's hard to see clarity way out there.*

# Chapter 101

*Saturday April 10th 1993*

*It's early Saturday morning, last night was different, it was really good, stark contrast to preceding days, it's so weird life can be all over the place.*

*Last night we were at the Opening Day for the Texas Rangers, their last year at Arlington Stadium. Nolan Ryan was a starter, also his last year, and he was stretching right in front of us. It was a great game between the Rangers and Boston, Nolan Ryan got the win. Jose Canseco was starting in right field and he turned around and he waved at Tracy. Imagine that for a future story. He also smacked a homerun, it was awesome, Rangers won 3-1. I told Tracy he was waving at me. There were 12 of us there to witness this last Opening Day, it was real live great fun. Katie and Mark were there, but they forgot their tickets. After the game I was detained by a policeman. I was trying to find my way out in the stadium parking lot along with about 40,000 other people. Tracy was guiding me out, she saw the left turn after I passed it. She shrieks "turn around,"*

*I do. I turn around in the middle of the street and almost hit a policeman. He was burning mad, "Stop", he told me loudly to "wait over there", I thought he meant the other side of the street, so I do another u turn, ended up in a 360', where I waited. He comes over with his book and he wants to know what is going on. I told him I have no idea. I told him I didn't know where I was going. That Tracy was trying to guide us home and we have 6 kids who just saw Nolen Ryan. I told him I messed up. He let us go, mostly because we hadn't been drinking. Off we merrily went, farther down the street, Tracy shrieks I missed the turn, I have to do the same thing. I turn around in the middle of the street and guess what.. off we go.*

*It was a kick, we all had a lot of fun and lots of laughter. It's weird, the fun and the laughter you are able to experience.*

*When I got home Betty was miraculously up. Waiting for me. How does this stuff happen so down, close to the bottom, and then she's up? Two days before she spent the day like she did with the nurses and now. I couldn't believe that she was up, standing in front of me. We sat for a little while and visited. It was really nice, she was so calm. It's just so weird that things can be so intense and so crazy and then so calm again.*

*We didn't stay up too long, tomorrow we will be greeted at 7:00 in the morning by a nurse who will be here 8 hours a day, 7 days a week.*

*Betty's insurance policy says she's approved for 4 hours of home nursing care a week! I don't get it? There are 192 hours in a week, what is 4 hours, do they come for 30 minutes each day? Dumb, 4 hours was nothing. Now we have 8 hours a day. How did this happen?*

*I think part of it was that the nurses were so freaked out the day before, and they are not sure where they want Betty to be. I think they want to contain Betty's exposure. It was a huge thing for them. I remember once thinking of being hesitant around Betty and AIDS. It never manifested. HIV was never a consideration, not at clinics, not at the Food Pantry and never around Betty. I never have thought whether I would get HIV. It wasn't something that came into play, it didn't stop any interaction. We were safe. It was always Betty, that's all we saw. It was all Tracy saw, Betty was there.*

*I don't know. We followed safeguards described by nurses, doctors. But golly, HIV is there, really fast, body fluids, everything you can think of could be there so fast, and you're reacting while responding, one has to be faster than the other.*

*I'm thinking 75% is with me on this.*

*It seems like it would be a matter of days or weeks, but*

*I think this will be the ride we are taken on, very intense parts and then lulls, and then this would become months. It would be so much better to have a nurse here. We can't go another way.*

*A nursing home or hospital won't work.*

*And the nurses rightfully saw that it would be very difficult for us to take care of Betty alone.*

*So there we were late at night, after Opening Day, in Betty's room, preparing for a nurse, 8 hours a day beginning tomorrow. Betty was a little uncomfortable with this. She wants us or herself to take care of her, and there is a percentage of time where we can and my God we have seen when we can't.*

# Chapter 102


*Saturday, April 10, 1993*

*Busy day today, good day. A nurse was here today. It went well, some associated anxiety.*

*It's now late Saturday night. I'm about to go to sleep but I wasn't able to sleep and I'm lying here in the darkness. You know what one of the things that was scaring me and keeping me awake? Fear. Fear from wondering where Jenny was at 10:30 last night when I called, it was a Friday night, and I was bothered by the thought. And it is funny and I'm dumb, because it would have been ok for me to do the same thing I was imagining Jenny probably not doing on a Friday night!*

# Chapter 103

*Sunday morning, April 11th 1993*

*I may have gotten on the plane too early, we're still getting ready to go but I wanted to make sure I was on. Yesterday was good. I'm not sure where I'd rather be, Denver or Dallas? Dallas.*

*The pilot just announced that Denver is an hour earlier, how can anything be earlier than this?*

*Still hung up on the Friday night that was never real. It took me over 100 reasons I could think of to soothe me into a deep sleep. Fear and paranoia. Fear comes from real stuff. Fear comes from real monsters. Paranoia, the monsters aren't real, we create them. Not quite the same thing, one's real the other is not, more weird realities. How do you know which one you are in?*

# Chapter 104

*Saturday, May 29, 1993*

*Hello,*

*Tomorrow I fly to Dallas. I was excited about writing about the past month, stuff like working, sub jobs, Jenny, Ryan, Tess, Betty, everything that mattered the last month doesn't seem to matter as much now. Can't even really remember what I've been doing the past month, only know what I got now. Things aren't too bad.*

*The school year ended pretty well. Spent most of the month subbing at one job in Jeffco. I have two strong possibilities that if I follow up hard they could lead to really good jobs. One's in Jefferson County and one's in Englewood.*

*Jenny and I have had some connections on a heart level, more from remembered moments. Probably stronger disconnections on an emotional level and then a mix up on the thought level. Anyway, that is where it is at with Jenny, not much has changed. We live apart and when we see each other we interact. It's not making a connection, not necessarily adding to the disconnect. The disconnect is over, severed almost. You know it is like sometimes I make a movement or think about some action to move us toward some acceptance of one another. Other times I feel strong against such an idea, and would rather go with this and see where we go. I don't know, I'm lost somewhere on this one. Maybe the timing is wrong.*

*So things here are looking pretty good, good possibility of a job, comfortable with where Jenny and I are. And tomorrow I will go see Betty. Guess who just showed up?*

# Chapter 105

*Sunday, May 30, 1993*

*It's been a pretty funny day. I woke up at 7:30 a.m. this morning in Denver, plenty early, had a big breakfast, made cookies, cut the grass, walked around with Linda, had lunch with Jenny, sold cookies with the Ryan and Tess on Gaylord Street during the fair, drove to the Stapleton Airport with Linda, flew to Dallas, laughed and laughed at Tracy's, came to Betty's, sat around with Big Mike. Oh, I did the wash, watered the grass, packed my suitcase, made more cookies for the girls to sell, talked with Uncle Al, went to the Gaylord Street Fair, bought some lucky beads, that I still have with me, went to the bank, was picked up at DFW by Tracy, Maureen and Katie, played football with the kids, watch some TV with Big Mike and now it is heading to midnight and I'm heading to bed, good thing I had an extra hour.*

# Chapter 106

*Memorial Day May 31st 1993*

*One more day until June. June already. It seems I missed some days or they just went right past me. Nothing is waiting for me to do it. How it passes is how it's done. It's been crazy and it has worked well.*

*So far I've only seen Betty lying in bed sleeping. The sound of her breath is heavy and comfortable. Right before Ally dropped me off she told me to listen for Betty because she's been getting up and falling. Big Mike describes Betty as being incoherent and incredibly sad. He described one recent night that Betty woke up and not knowing what to do or where she was, she went out to the kitchen. She was sitting in the kitchen trying hard to sort out what she was supposed to be doing, she sat there literally not knowing what she was doing. Betty thought she ought to be cleaning and in mid sentence her thoughts would flip to something different, what she was doing was forgotten. Betty told Big Mike she had to pack her things and get ready for a trip with Harry. But before that she needed to go out and find a dog that had run away many years ago from our house in Westport, Conn.*

*These are the things left undone and there's no time left.*

*Big Mike told of the other day when while they were sitting in the den, he had to get up and do something. He had Betty promise she wouldn't get up and leave the couch till he came back. Betty got up and started wandering, bewildered, from her bedroom to the couch talking to herself. Telling herself things she needs to do with her mother before she left. Big Mike said he listened and tried to help her do things.*

# Chapter 107

*Hello, still here.*

*Last time I was here, Betty started home nursing care for 8 hours a day and it has been the best thing in the world. I have heard such fondness by Betty when she talks about Mary. There have been days when the nurses have stayed and they were times when they were here for 24 hours. Last Sunday Betty was even sicker than ever. For 5 days she was unable to get out of bed, unable to eat, unable to do anything, hardly able to move, like bed care. There's no way it could have been any other way. I don't know if we could imagine what it would have been like with no nursing care because I don't think that is something that would ever have happened. They have been amazing.*

*Tracy has been here every day almost all day long. She's amazing. She's fearless.*

*There are mother daughter bonds. Betty and Tracy's is*

*endless. I keep seeing it. It's hard to explain. They were close growing up, they were both young. What they have absolutely doesn't waver. And it's more than this, they're connected somehow, they know what each are thinking, they feel each other's feelings, the depths of each other's sadness and pain, Tracy feels it. I don't know.*

*They are both thankful for each other, they're thankful for what they each do for each other, and they're thankful to be around each other.*

*Tomorrow at 1:00 p.m., Head nurse Donna and her supervisor are coming to talk about Betty's care. They said they have things they need to talk about. How the care is going, is it taking care of Betty? And the cost of the nursing care that the insurance is paying for is a lot more than what is in the policy, it's way out of policy. I like way out. They initially thought that Betty would only live a couple weeks past the day in April when they approved the 8 hours of nursing care. Well she has, and now they're wondering what they did and what to do next. We're a little concerned that the insurance company wants to cut the care to an aide, 4 days a week and we would be responsible for more hours. 4 hours would be like they're here from 8:00 a.m. to noon, and then from noon until the next morning we would take care of Betty or out of pocket. A couple things about this sounds a little too much or not enough. We have also heard that they may want to send Betty to a nursing home where there is more cost effective treatment.*

# Chapter 108

*Tuesday, June 1st, 1993*

*Hello "is there anybody out there?"*

*We had a meeting today with Donna and her supervisor. Donna comes out weekly to see Betty and checks on how she is doing. Donna said she stays in contact with the nurse and together they compiled notes on Betty's care. The meeting began with Donna. Using her notes, Donna told us what's been going on with Betty and what her symptoms were. Betty vomits almost daily, diarrhea 2-3 times a week, she has significant pain daily. Betty can't get out of bed most days, she sleeps, she's not able to eat daily. When Betty talks it is rambling and nonsense stories, they call this part, dimensional or something, otherwise Betty doesn't talk. She cries each day. Donna laid it out all in pretty graphic terms. She described the level of care that is needed on a daily basis as continual acute care. Donna said these symptoms would continue and get much much worse as Betty continues to waste away. That's the part that will blow us all away. I hate that. I hate the wasting away shit.*

*They talked about the long list of medication that Betty was on, the continual administration of meds and flushing the port. Donna was so frank and direct it shocked and terrified everyone including her supervisor. The suffering and pain, the personal hygiene, the dignity, it was unbelievable, it was unreal. Donna. It was hard to hear, it was all you could hear. Death can be horrifying.*

*After Donna we talked about Betty and where we saw her. I spoke about how hard it is each day for Betty to suffer like Donna just described. How each day we see it and feel it. About how hard it is for us to see her dying daily, how slow it seems, right there everyday that Betty is alive she's dying, every moment she is alive is a moment closer to death.*

*Betty's our mother. She wants to die here.*

*I'm not necessarily sure that they came with a directive or anything like an ultimatum.*

*I think more they wanted to share information and gather information, see where we were at and consider the future. They did more than that. At the end of the meeting Donna and her supervisor agreed to approach the insurance company with the recommendation that a nurse be here for 8 hours a day and an aide be here with Betty for 4 hours a day, 12 hours. Excellent.*

*Way beyond the most important meeting there was.*

*Ally was there, she left in tears, she was crying hard in her whole body. I held her, she was tight and tense, tight like it would burst, tight like everything was covered and you wanted to scream out, a scream that no one will hear. Big Mike went to the back porch, he was horrified at the amount of Betty's suffering. It's like we each do what we do with Betty and it's not all shared. If we were to share we would fill a hole, at least we come and go, not Betty, she's there for all of it, she'll be buried in it.*

*Big Mike was freaked, the thought about the suffering and pain that Betty is going through, he may. Scary. He's hardly believing what it is like, and it is out there waiting for him. Geez, what that must be like?*

# Chapter 109

*Hello, in the backyard. There are times like this that are so peaceful it seems like how can it be like this when it's like that? So unreal. These times come to help you.*

*There are hundreds of little bits of cotton from the big cottonwood tree, gliding around the backyard like they are alive and here for your enjoyment. Hundreds of them, dancing around the backyard, I may join them. The shade trees are laying shadows across the yard and there's a slight gentle breeze blowing the chimes for the birds to sing to.*

*Two chimes and a blue jay..*

# Chapter 110

*Wednesday morning, June 2nd, 1993*

*The nice thing about Dallas is there are deep lulls where everything is quiet and peaceful. Even Foo Foo is sitting quietly on the porch; he's usually nuts, jumping up and down and then running around and around in circles. It's like a respite, a pit stop, we've all had pit stops, it's a relief.*

*Last night the basketball game was exciting, Game 5, Sonic's 114, Suns 120, Barkley had 43 pts, how do you do that? Good game.*

*My chicken enchiladas were great, if you ever want to know the recipe, let me know. The hot tub was really nice, ice cream and brownies were delicious, apple biscuits, orange sliced tea, it was a nice night.*

*Later*

*I'm resting in the backyard, there are more dancing*

*fairies, lots of shade, nice breeze, the chimes and bluejays are calling back and forth to each other. What happens to everything here, I guess it all continues, a new cast, new set design and it starts over again.*

*We'll all be gone.*

*I was just in Betty's room. She hasn't fallen asleep for a little over an hour. She started talking. Some of it is sad and some is a bit funny. It goes around and around as she sees a purse for sale cheaper than the one at the party that all these people have come to. It's a party for her, and they are here to see her, but she was hiding her secret and after she throws water on him, he never said anything after that about her secret.*

*Betty started making something with her hands, folding a tissue and Mary knelt beside her. When she was done folding the tissue she gave it to Mary and told her to put it away so the kids don't see it. All this was happening as if that was all that was happening anywhere.*

*I came outside, there's a robin chirping loudly, the chimes are blowing in the wind, birds are racing through the sky and I think I'm close to heaven. She's back.*

*A light brown dove landed in the grass and walked slowly to the sidewalk, but didn't get on the sidewalk. It was joined by a white dove, and they stood there looking at me, then they gently went into flight and landed on a branch where they have been ever since. Waiting. They're messengers, bringing their tales of love and compassion. Suddenly they left, just like Betty said they would when the party was over.*

# Chapter 111

*Someday after.*

*I was sitting on Betty's bed. She was talking about the color of the room changing from pink to gray and when she wakes up she sees a pink wall and on the wall is a doorknob and in there, back in there is the gray room empty, with only a big box on the ground. Then she starts to cry and for a couple of minutes the room seems all white, there are no walls, there's only one way out that leads nowhere.*

*Betty says she is doing okay with the progression of AIDS. She says she's okay with the pain, she's okay with her mind going, she wants to know how Big Mike is. She says it's time to get ready for a party on Irvin Simmons so she will talk to me tomorrow. The stories bumping along toward somewhere, or maybe nowhere.*

*Betty says that we are scared of death, scared to death*

*of it. She wants to talk about it with each of us, she wants to say goodbye to each of us, personally, as close as she can get to each of us, she wants that time. She wants to tell each of us how much she loves us, she wants us to know we were her life. Then she closed her eyes and went to the party.*

*We are scared, I'm scared. I'm still trying to hang on to something else about her, it's the past. There's the past and the present with Betty, not much time in the future. The past was wonderful in so many ways. The present, the wonderful is down to moments, minutes that are often intense, pitched sharply to the very end corner of love. It's in this place where all the wonder, all the joy, all the love you had with a person, comes together in a corner of love. It's immense, it's pure, it burns forever in the corner of your heart.*

# Chapter 112



*Friday, June 4th, 1993*

*I'm sitting on the side of the hot tub soaking up the early morning sun, before long the breeze will stop and the temperature will head past the 90's.*

*Betty has hardly spoken. It's hard for her to sit up, she can't really get out of bed, when she does, she can't walk by herself, when she does get somewhere, she can't manage by herself and needs someone.*

*Whoever is here will help Betty get everywhere and will help her with everything she does. Earlier she was sitting on the couch, her head was back, her eyes were closed, her mouth was open, she was sort of gasping for air, big long gasps for air that would visibly shutter her chest. Then it was followed by no breathing and peace. Shutterfulness followed by peacefulness.*

*From across the room I would follow her breath and then using my mind I'd try to coax her into resting and letting go. Letting go?*

*Couldn't do it. I bet you could though. You get the rhythm, the beat, your breaths becoming one breath. Tracy could probably do it with Betty.*

# Chapter 113

*Friday, June 4th, 1993*

*It's in the morning that began with Betty being very, very sick. She can just barely talk, it's a very low voice, hardly even a whisper. She quietly said that she was very sick and she wants to feel better. She said the pain was everywhere, her hip hurt, the bottom of her stomach hurt, her back hurt, the pain was all over her. Then she started to cry.*

*Why is there so much pain?*

*Later*

*It's in the afternoon. Earlier people came by today to see Betty. I faded away.*

*Tracy, Nick and Emma and Ally and a baby, and then Joyce and Dale stopped by.*

*For each visitor Betty would have on a nightgown, be*

*propped up in her bed, her hair smoothed. No sign of what happens here, it's crazy. Betty could sit there, listen and respond. She looked good, it's the present not the past.*

*First with Joyce and then with Dale, there were chilling responses or no answers to our questions. Dale was moved. My eyes swelled with tears listening to Dale. Dale said that there would be a sign or a flag that will go up and we will see it, it'll be something more than what it's been, more shocking, more painful, more non-person. Dale said once you see that sign, once you pass that sign there is no return. He said we would see it and we would know.*

# Chapter 114

*Friday evening*

*I was over at Ally's this evening and we are talking about all the fun and laughter that Betty had recently at Mother's Day, a little more than a month ago. It made me cry. I had to keep getting up and walking around to try and stop the tears. I just kept crying whenever we started to talk about Betty and we would wonder if we would see her up and around again. Just like they say you have to love each day like it's your last, you don't know when that last day will be here. The last day doesn't always end in death. The last day is the last time it happens. Sometimes we don't even know it will be the last time. If I had known that that was the last night with Jenny.*

*Things are over when it passes and may not have a happening to end it.*

# Chapter 115

*Saturday morning, June 5th, 1993*

*Very early this morning, in the wee hours of this day, when there is very little light, while I was sleeping, I heard Betty crying and got up. I went into her room. Her feet were swung over the side of her bed, but her body was still laying down, her upper body had pinned her left arm to the bed and she needed her arm so that she could push herself up. She couldn't move. Her arm was numb, it was hurting and she was crying. I went over and touched her on her shoulder, she was drenched with sweat, her back was sweating, her head was a mass of wet hair, beads of sweat covering her face that was red. She was so frightened and so scared she was crying. Her eyes, frantic, searching all around the room for something, anything, anything that could save her. She was crying, she said she wanted to go home, she didn't want to be wherever she was, she wanted to go home, away from here. I had moved her body up off her arm and she was sitting up. I was holding her from falling over. She was exhausted. She couldn't stop crying.*

*She had to go to the bathroom. And when I stood her up she collapsed on her legs and into my arms. I held her for as long as I could. Her head resting on my shoulder and she was crying. We sat back down on the bed, I called for Big Mike. From the front and the back, with torment and pain, we moved Betty into the bathroom. It is unreal.*

*It seems if you use words to describe an experience, your words limit what it was, there are no words.*

# Chapter 116

*Everything is back to normal, Betty is back in bed. It's still dark, I laid there until she fell back to sleep. In the darkness my thoughts and feelings become ghosts, floating by in front of me. I thought I was electrified, it was all so shocking.*

*It happened again, same morning. It was still early, I was still in bed and I heard Betty again. At first I thought I heard her walking down the hall and she was talking. She wasn't in the hall, she was on the bathroom floor, she was as completely wiped out as you can be. It was totally unreal how she was there with seemingly almost nothing left of herself. There was no physical strength. She couldn't make any thoughtful connection with anything, nothing. The feelings and emotions she was having were beyond her capacity to understand. She was lying on the bathroom floor except everything about her was wiped out. There was an instinct to survive, to save herself. She was crawling on the bathroom floor trying to do something, she was crying, she wanted to go home.*

*Woke up Big Mike, and we gently lifted Betty up, cleaned her up, cooled her down, got her back into bed, covered her up and for the past 2 hours, Betty's been lying there crying and sweating. She said that she had something very important to talk to me about. She has been unable to say anything, trying to say it for the past 2 hours. She will later.*

*And then you know what happened? Big Mike was leaning over Betty, close to her, almost like to give her a hug, and Betty grabbed his collar and brought him even closer. Everything stopped. Everything was quiet. Betty said "you did this to me and I trusted you." Big Mike tried to pull back, but she held him, she had saved an oz. of strength for this. He saw something, heard something and he was shocked, then he froze, couldn't move, wasn't allowed to. All he could do was accept it. He stared into Betty's eyes, and did. Then she saved him, saying something else.*

*What Betty said was clear, what it meant was clear and how it happened was clear. Big Mike knows. He knows what he did. Mother f*****.*

*I left the room and I came outside. My chest was so constricted I couldn't breathe. Gasped for air, huge heaves of breath.*

*Now I'm sitting in the backyard. Betty is falling asleep, gone, exhausted by the struggle to survive. She will sleep to face it again when she awakes. Me? On top.*

# Chapter 117



*Sunday afternoon*

*Tired.*

*I wish somewhere there was someone waiting for me to return. Upon returning we walk quietly, no word. Hand in hand, we would walk to nowhere, there would be no end to our walk and no end to our love.*

# Chapter 118

*Sunday night*

*Betty is asleep. You want to know something? After almost 3 days of no eating, no strength, unable to walk, inaudible speech, immense pain and sadness, Betty woke and she was wondering where she had been. She wanted to know what had been going on. Where was she? She wanted to know how she hurt herself, and how she got here. Was she in a car wreck or was she mugged in an alley? Where has she been? Betty didn't know. I don't think it was a car wreck but I do feel exhausted from the ride of the last couple days that go up and down and back down and down, and nobody knows where you've been. This is amazing.*

*Earlier Betty was able to get up and walk with minimal assistance. She talks and is coherent about the things around her, the walls aren't moving and pink. And she has minor pain. It was just as unreal as the last couple days. My head goes around and around wondering the same thing as Betty. Where has she been? She must go way out there, sees what it's like and comes back. Maybe her soul goes off searching, and leaves the body with no form, direction or sense.*

*Betty talked for quite a while, most of it was good, bits of other parts were inside out, upside down and in circles. The things that Betty talks about, all really happened, it's all real. When the things happened are not in the right order but they really did happen. Maybe time doesn't matter anymore, but these things do. It matters more that it happened. Maybe things go together better in the order Betty puts them in. It is all real stuff. I follow her stories through time and they flow through dreams and reality.*

# Chapter 119

*Tuesday night, June 8th, 1993*

*I leave on Thursday June 10th.*

*Yesterday, Monday wasn't too bad. Betty was feeling okay, her stories were heading out there, bit wild.*

*Tracy and I took her to see Dr. Pounders. He asked how things were. He knows how things are. You don't really have to explain. So much of this is emotional or thoughtful, and you may or may not be able to explain that. He'll look at the medication for adjustments, it's hard to manage with the spikes in symptoms. He did a blood test to see if she still has HIV, we think any f****** day now this is going to go away, and we will.*

*On the way home we decided to stop at Braum's Ice Cream. The drive was sort of funny. We'd all be talking and Betty would say things out of the blue or give funny answers to questions. When we got to*

*Braum's and we started to order, Betty was reading pictures of food on the windows for her order. She ordered a club sandwich, an ice cream cone and a sherbert. We figured she was doing the same thing while we were driving. Betty would see a word or phrase and mold the words into her thoughts and responses. Pretty funny. Maybe not?*

*Last night I went to Nick's baseball game. His team is playing the Royals, who were coached by my old high school friend Deco. Deco always went for the most fun, he liked the big laughing kicks. His personality was bigger than life, 10 times bigger than mine. I was probably accepted more when I was hanging out with him. I heard something once, how this bigger than life personality, would alter a thing in his life because he didn't want to be made fun of. There are things about us, to a degree how we are, to a degree how we look, the things we don't control, are as much about us, and these things stop us. And me and you, we each have 1,2,3...things about us that stop us. I don't want to be judged.*

*He's here now, coaching, helping, volunteering, he was like that. His parents were there, it was cool to see someone who really cared about us when we were young, and they still cared. They were always nice, they never bothered us, they gave us a lot of room to enjoy ourselves and they always fed us. The night was fun and I'm always amazed at the extremes that we live in. It's like all the emotions and feelings are set on fire and you get away.*

*I got home about 10:00 p.m. and Betty was awake, standing in the dark, with a knife, over Big Mike who was sleeping in his bed. It was almost ghostly, her long gown looked like a drape that hung and made her seem to be almost floating. Betty was a glow in the darkness. And she said "time to wake up Mike, it's time to go."*

*Sorry, I added the knife part.*

*There she was, standing there whispering for Mike to*

*wake. I sort of startled her a little, and she moved toward me. She said she couldn't sleep. We went out to the kitchen and fixed a snack. Sherbert, licorice, orange slices and hot tea. Pretty wild stuff, but it all came to life as we talked. The sherbert was like eating ice cream as a kid, the licorice was Good and Plenty that Betty would always bring me when I was sick, the orange slices Betty's mother, Laddie would always eat, the hot tea was calmness. Things you would find on a HIV menu. Sitting there eating junk was a gentle ride in a quiet boat around a dark lake, the sights, the smells, everything was familiar and real. We enjoyed the snack, watched a little bit of Jay Leno and about 11:30 Betty said she was tired and ready to sleep.*

*It went from Thursday morning to Saturday afternoon where Betty could not walk and talk and eat. Then from Saturday afternoon to Monday night, she could walk, talk and eat. Today Tuesday she has slowed down. She slept till about 11:00 and then had breakfast. She ate pretty well, then slept on the couch from noon till 3:30. She ate a little, and then from 3:45 till 5:00 she slept in her bed, then she woke up.*

*She was rested, and got ready for a barbecue.*

*Big Mike, Ally, Tracy, Nick, Ben, Daniel, Spike, Emma we're here. Betty was dressed, she perked up quite a bit and was so happy to see everyone. She loved having everyone around her, especially the little kids, she loves them. She loves Spike and she thinks he's the cutest littlest kid she's ever seen. Betty puts everything she has out for the grandkids, knick knacks to play with, coloring books, little crafts from Michaels, all sorts of little things that they can do. It makes her as happy as they are, it makes her feel better, smiling and laughing, she was so alive.*

# Chapter 120

*Wednesday, June 9th, 1993*

*Tomorrow I leave. I wish I wasn't. I'd rather have this life. It's crazy going from one place to another.*

*We got a wheelchair for Betty. 'Hi there, here's your wheelchair, this is how you get around, this will take you from here to there, where you won't need it'*

# Chapter 121

*Thursday, June 10th, 1993*

*Dear Jean,*

*I'm writing to someone, so that I'm not writing to myself.*

*It's Thursday morning at DFW airport. I had two pens with no ink and just paid $10.06 for a medium blue pen, the fancy Cowboy pens are $26.*

*Thunder, lightning and rain have delayed the arrival of the plane from Houston that will take us to Denver. I have a nice seat at the gate and it looks like everyone is here. Talking is minimal, most people were either dropped off or their ride couldn't wait for the delay, had to be somewhere else. Most people don't know who they're sitting next to, so they read, mostly the newspaper, a couple people have magazines and one guy has a laptop. Other people are just sitting, wondering where they have been and where they're going.*

*I'm on the plane. There is a couple on the plane, sitting together, reading the news. The man has gray hair that is cut short, tan face, tan arms, in a mod shirt open halfway down showing his hairy chest and a gold chain announcing his desire for youthfulness. Next to him is his wife, she's tired from trying so hard to be young enough for this old stud. She has colored most of her gray hair, wears makeup, red lipstick and she's wearing an outfit that is better suited for the young and trim girl her husband so desires. They haven't spoken, they don't have much to say to each other anymore.*

*Last night I laid with Betty on her bed holding her hand, her long thin fingers, as soft and pretty as they have ever been. Betty is so pretty, her face, her hair, her deep green eyes, just beautiful.*

*We didn't speak, she may have been asleep, words were not used or needed, we laid there and unspokenly we said goodbye to each other. I will miss her everyday that I'm not here and will see her soon again.*

*Suffering, pain, terror, misery, sickness and death we give life to, they have no being, no power until we touch them, it is so hard not to.*

*The old stud read through the whole flight, landing, and while we taxied. He said nothing to his wife and now he is leading her out and she follows. Shit what if parts of him are me! Not the stud part.*

# Chapter 122

*Friday, June 26th, 1993*

*I just purchased my second $10.06 pen at the airport. I'm on my way to Dallas for the weekend. I arrived tonight around 10:30, the plane is delayed because of a thunderstorm in Dallas. Here I'll wait. This weekend is my 20th high school reunion.*

*20 years since I bounced out of Jesuit College Prep. They were real Jesuits teaching, with much the same thoughts as the infamous Jesuit of '60s and '70s. I'm grateful and fortunate. I never thought too much about after get high school. I thought after childhood, elementary school, junior high, high school and college, that was all you had to do after that the pieces fall into place. Never thought of being an adult, maybe some don't, 50/50 people know what they will do, others have a vague sense of having a job, getting married and having kids. Those things sound great, it's when you add the details that it can become so much better and so much badder. There's so much more that you have to learn and experience after college. You have relationships that aren't supposed to end, and they do, you have jobs that aren't supposed to end, and they do. There are lives that aren't supposed to end and they do too. You pick up many broken pieces, you wonder how they shattered, and then you put back together again what you can, like Umpy. It's wild, I feel so young.*

*We were a strange little generation. We seem to have come at the end of everything, end of the boomers, end of the hippies, then stuck in there between the 60s and the '80s, we never became our parents' generation, each generation was to be better than previous generations. We were supposed to measure up to WWII vets, to use them as a measurement, not sure if we have, we didn't mature as our parents. Now we are the measurements of maturity and everyone can live up to that. Betty was younger than I was when we moved to Dallas. She was already a lady, a woman, a mother. She was entertaining parties of people, all at 35 years old. I couldn't have done that, I still want to be entertained. Maybe it's me..*

*We just landed. I'm waiting for 135 people in front of me to get off the plane. I'm sitting in the very backseat, last row. Harry always said the back is the safest, tail breaks off. The pilot had warned us of encountering Texas size winds and we sure did. Twice it felt like we dropped about a thousand feet, people screamed when we dropped, it was wild. I don't like airplane flights when people clap and cheer because we make it.*

# Chapter 123

*Saturday, June 27, 1993*

*I was sitting outside in the backyard eating breakfast while Betty was crying for me and I didn't hear her, they didn't know where I was, I wasn't available, I felt terrible, still do. Betty was in tears, sobbing because she thought she had been mean to me for being so sick and unable to eat the breakfast I had fixed for her. It takes two, I had to have given off that vibe. F***. I am how I am and at times it screams to be more.*

*Mary Bell found me outside and said Betty wanted me. When I walked into her room, Betty was sitting on the edge of the bed, crying. She opened her arms, spread her arms out far, her head to one side, like she was on a cross and she had died leaving all of us. It was like heaven. Betty took me into her arms and she said "I love you Wayne" and she held me close and she held me tight to her body and said "Wayne, we're not going to make it'*"

*She needed me to comfort her.*

*I'm crying and shaking, getting ready to take a shower and go to my 20th High School reunion picnic with my shiny white legs, me and Deco.*

*I don't get it, there's not always a flow to life. Put yourself on a river, maybe you have a destination. Look along the way, the forest, the beauty, the calm. Times you're traveling with others. The journey enhanced with the joy and love of others. And in front of you a bend, you may or may not see it coming. Right around the bend, Bam, f***, I don't know. The bam you heard could be anything of the stuff that comes our way. Some of our experiences are like rapids, they may be small, bothersome for a while, sometimes enough to knock you around a bit. They could get worse, smashing into you, you feel it, it's painful, it seems endless. When you come out of the bend, maybe someone is not with you any more, maybe someone* *said "f*** this" and they got off. Maybe you end up alone, maybe your destination changes or you know what, maybe everyone made it and each of you are stronger. Your love is stronger for making it. How do you get rid of some of the 'maybes'?*

# Chapter 124



*Sunday, June 27, 1993*

*Golly, I'm at the airport heading back to Denver. I can't believe it. Just seems so unreal to be here and now to be leaving. Too crazy.*

*I'm kneeling with my bags at DFW. It looks like a scene in R2D2 are too. The terminal is packed, wall to wall, no seats to wait. People are everywhere, they all look strange and are doing strange things. I'm on top. They just announced boarding for all rows to Frankfurt, Germany, I'm at the wrong gate, rats.*

*Made it and am on the plane.*

*You know it was wild, there was a janitor, the same janitor was at all three of the 20th High School reunion parties that I went to this weekend. The first night at a graduate's house, the janitor was sitting on the table in the garage. He was big, filling almost the whole table. He was just sitting there, not really talking to anyone and not doing any work. Then the next night at Ursuline Academy there was a formal party and the janitor was there in a suit! Dallas is crazy, the janitors wear suits. And then the most unbelievable thing, the janitor was at the Jesuit picnic. How did they get him to work all three events? He was there wearing the biggest shorts and the biggest shoes and he was sitting on another table talking to some of my old classmates. I thought okay, after 3 days working they have become friends and I thought that it was great. Later I was standing there talking to some friends and the janitor came up to me, said hello and he started talking to me about the picnic. I thought after the chit-chat he was going to ask me to help him clean something, but instead he looks at me real funny. Then he introduces himself as... of class of '73. I knew him! He was a much bigger deal than me.*

# Chapter 125

*Wednesday, July 28th 1993*

*It is Wednesday morning and I'm on a plane to Dallas. It was a month in Denver. Something is swirling wildly inside of me, I feel all out of sorts, nothing seems to be where it needs to be to be right. Leaving Denver is hard this time. Leaving Ryan and Tessa this time is hard. Everything seems hard.*

*From the phone calls it sounds like it's been hard for Betty. She hasn't been walking for days and more days. She hasn't been out of bed for days and days. She hardly talks, if she does it's hard to make sense. She's like losing her mind and I don't know.*

*Tomorrow there will be a meeting with Dr. Pounders, the nurses and the insurance company. They're all coming over to Betty's tomorrow. They want to know what we are going to do now? Time is up. And when they say that I'm going to scream. I'm going to scream from the depths of my being, from the darkest place, I'll scream "No" They want decisions made about Betty. The doctor will give us a prognosis, the nurses will recount their observations, the insurance will want to cut costs. Then we will talk for Betty.*

*We have to let go more of Betty. We don't want to let go and we have to. We will run out of time if we don't. We need to move into a different place with Betty. It will be the last place we go with Betty. All the places you've been with someone this will be the last. The journey ends here, in this place, in this room surrounded by endless love.*

*Betty may be close to when she had it in her mind. She didn't really want all the antibiotics fighting off the viruses and infections. She didn't want the TPN to be her food that kept her alive. And the pain far exceeds what she ever wanted to bear.*

*It's always so easier to say when, when it is some other time, it is easier to say now when it is not now. It's*

*Betty's decision, we know what she wants and that's what I hope we get.*

# Chapter 126



*This bed is so comfortable. I took a 3-hour nap today when I got to Betty's. I was so tired. Maybe it was from being at Elitch's last night in Denver, or maybe from the heat, it is so hot here. I'm sharing this bed with three bears and a white rabbit. I'm listening to Betty's breathing over the monitor, the inhale is a short gasp, the exhale is relief, it's mine. It's my night to listen to Betty, listen to her breathing and if she tries to get up.*

*Things felt so nice when I first came into Betty's room earlier. There are comfortable chairs and pillows. Flowers were around the room, pictures and knick-knacks on the dresser. There were things that meant something to her. There was light and color, it was really, really nice, it was like walking into a dream. In the middle of the room was a big hospital bed and in the bed was Betty. She was curled up toward one side of the bed, she looked small, thin, an outline under the sheets. Her legs didn't seem to reach as far down the bed. She looked good, good color, her hair was thick, red around the eyes, her face was more narrow. I looked at her and she woke up. I felt so much love from her come over me.*

*The next couple hours I was in and out of the room. I would leave to catch my breath, going down the hall through the den to the backyard or into the kitchen. I'd cry, sometimes laugh. It is a trail, more of a trial, to follow Betty's conversation. She talked quite a bit, only three times was it clear and lucid what she was talking about. The first time she asked if I had talked to Jeff. Betty wanted to know if we had stopped fighting. Not sure where that came from, the past or present. The second time she said something about dying. She said she doesn't want to live but she didn't want to die and leave everyone. The third time she made sense I forgot what she was talking about. The rest of the time she would talk about fragments of her life that happened but she'd put them in an order that really didn't go together. She couldn't remember when she was in love, "I can't remember being in love." Parts of her childhood had faded also. Or it would be someone doing somebody else's something somewhere they didn't do it. And then Betty would laugh and chuckle and think it was the funniest thing that everything was mixed up like that, she liked it mixed up. One time she looked at me, did a double take and laughed a short little laugh. Tracy probably did that. The whole scene was really nice and keeps us away from where she is.*

*It's crazy the parts of us we lose, parts that made us whole, are forgotten.*

# Chapter 127

*Thursday, July 29th, 1993*

*It's night time.*

*A big cockroach just chased me out of the kitchen.*

*Earlier there were three clowns in Betty's room.*

*The meeting was today. Things happened so quickly, it was such a short meeting.*

*I remember thinking how fast it passed and was over. A lifetime stuffed in a thimble.*

*When it was over I got up and went to sit with Betty. While I was sitting there I was seeing and feeling how the decisions that were made had turned quickly into a reality that was light years away from the decision. The decision doesn't match the reality. What they decided will fill a spot but not the whole picture.*

*Ally left the meeting early, she was crying and nothing was going to stop her from getting away from it. Big Mike was very quiet and at one point when the nurses were talking about what to expect will happen to Betty, Big Mike was on the edge of his seat, holding his stomach, his face was white, all his color left him and it was just the beginning. He may have seen a ghost.*

*The meeting was to talk about the next stage of Betty's care. They made it sound pretty light and friendly when they called last week to set up the meeting. It sure the f*** wasn't light or friendly. The insurance company had a plan. They wanted the antibiotics to be stopped, they were okay with the virus or infection ravaging Betty's body. They wanted the TPN to be stopped, they were okay with Betty wasting away. They wanted the AZT to be stopped, they were okay with the HIV spreading. Anything that was fighting a virus they wanted stopped, anything that was aiding Betty's health they wanted stopped and then everything to stop the pain would be jacked up to the sky, Betty would be* *so high "she won't even feel a thing."*

*Eleanor, Betty's nurse, was torn between how personal it had become and the professional reality. Eleanor carries Spike and Emma so Betty can see them. She holds us when we can't stop shaking. She comforts Betty with her voice and her touch. Dr Pounders was there and he would have agreed to wait or would have agreed that we are now there and it was time to talk about pain management.*

*I went back to Betty's room a couple times during the meeting to hopefully make my heart lighter. Betty was unable to distinguish what she wanted to do. Betty do you want to stop everything? 'You won't even feel a thing' She wants someone else to decide, she's decided, she doesn't want to know. Somewhere in there she wasn't quite ready. I don't think she wants everything stopped. That's the part that has always scared her, wasting away, loss of dignity and humanness. She wants to stay here with us, she wants to see each of us, she wants to love Spike and Emma forever.*

*It has changed light years to say when, when Betty was further from death.*

*Weeks, months ago, any thought, any ideas, promises, they were made in the context of the day. They were one thing back then, it was easier to think that you would do anything to help Betty die how she wants. Part of it was the distance, part of it was for comfort. Betty wanted to know that she'd still be who she was when she died, she didn't want to waste away. But now, it's become more than comfort. It's becoming two completely different actions. What it is becoming is beyond what we do.*

*There are no words.*

# Chapter 128

*Friday, July 30th, 1993*

*Sitting with Betty and she says:*

*"Are Dick and Carol here?"*

*"Little girl, do you need help?"*

*"Boy, we could really have fun here."*

*"I'm glad I'm going soon."*

*"Do you know mom and sister cremated us."*

*"I think I've been at the wrong house, where am I?"*

*"Excuse me you haven't seen two girls dressed up as clowns have you?"*

*"Have you been out to see how the rooms are, if they're ready?"*

*"How much are you going to give me?"*

*"Are those men still here?"*

*"I want so much to go home."*

*What a day, hard to imagine that it all went on today and it's only 1:00 p.m.*

*I woke up real early. I didn't hear anything in the house and was able to go back to sleep till 9:00.*

*When I first woke up I sat with Betty. The conversation took us everywhere. Tula came in and said the insurance company was only approving 8 hours of nursing care a day, nothing on the weekend. Right after Tula, Janet called. Janet represents the insurance company. She's been in touch with us before about nursing care. Janet has always been fair and she has done a lot for us. I thank her. She reiterated that the nursing care we have had for 4 months has been way out of policy, and proceeded to 'highlight' what we talked about yesterday. In the next few days Betty will have medicine and nutrients stopped, and we will start pain management. 8 hours a day, no weekends, the nursing care is not needed as much. "We want your mom to be comfortable, with no pain."*

*I asked if there was any way we could get more hours to help while we are moving into this level of care. Janet said she would check into it and call me back. Then Tracy called, she was mad and really sad. She was frustrated, she was scared, she was crying, and all she cared about was Betty. How will mom be, will she know? Tracy didn't ask about how 'we' will do it, or what are 'we' going to do. 'We' didn't matter to Tracy, only Betty did.*

*Janet beeped in while Tracy was crying and said we were approved for 10 hours a day, no weekends.*

*Now it is just past 2:00, things just continue rolling in, rolling down, more nurses call, Big Mike calls, Laurie calls, Betty awakes and Tracy stops by.*

*I'm tired, I feel empty. It's weird, being tired,*

*exhausted, empty, you expel all that you have, all the capacity you have is used up. Then the body, the mind does an amazing thing, fills you back up. The exhausted time is when you're getting it back together, it's quiet and your capacity is refilling. Tiredness doesn't keep you from doing what you need to do, it gets you ready to answer the bell. And the phone keeps ringing. It's probably Big Mike with another idea of what needs to be done. Three more times it rings while I lay here I hear bells in my dreams.*

*It's much later now. I wanted to write to tell Ryan and Tess I saw a moondance tonight. It was almost a full moon. I was on top, floating in the air while in the hot tub. If you look into the pool of water, the reflection splits the moon. Two Moons were dancing side by side in the water. There's a gentle breeze and it is all you can hear, the trees blowing in the wind and the chimes singing. It is so calm sitting in the moonlight.*

*I feel rested, mentally, nothing there. Tracy says it's like this everyday and I believe her. Whatever I'm doing here, when I'm not here, it's almost all Tracy. It's unreal. She and Dan think I'm a weenie cuz I get up late and rest during the day.*

# Chapter 129

*Sunday night, August 1st, 1993*

*I just wrote the girls a letter. It's very late, very quiet and from nowhere I could hear Betty in a very soft voice calling out for Big Mike. It was barely a whisper. She was calling for Big Mike to come with her. She got me instead. I went into the room, she was in a dream, calling for Mike to join her. I sat on the side of her bed and held her hand. Her eyes would gently open for a moment and then close. Sometimes before her eyes were fully closed, they would roll back in her head and you could see nothing but the light hitting the white. Her body would shiver, sharp little movements.*

*You feel something sitting there so close to her. Like there were two of us going down to one of us. I don't know, whatever I say you have to try for yourself. Sit close to a dying person who's close to you. We all believe in something, even if you believe in nothing, it becomes something. I hope Betty passed me part of her heart, the part about how she treats her kids. I want to be like that. We were there for a long time connecting however you connect without talking, with touch and soulful. Time passes with nothing else in the room or seemingly in the world.*

# Chapter 130

*Monday, August 2, 1993*

*I remember sometime ago thinking that August was the month.*

*There was no end to Sunday, it went right into Monday and now it's 6 pm and it still hasn't ended. At 6:30, 30 minutes, Tracy and I are going to Plano General Hospital to see Big Mike.*

*He's there. We will talk to his doctor about how Big Mike went from healthy living to barely living during the past 24 hours. It started yesterday, Sunday, when Big Mike was at church or maybe it started this past Thursday during the meeting when Dr Pounders was telling us how Betty may die. It was then that Big Mike was holding his stomach and turned white. Then yesterday Big Mike came home from church, changed. He went to bed really early, he said he wasn't feeling well. I stayed up with Betty until about 2:00 this morning. Betty would wake up during the night and she would start to talk and we'd visit like old friends. It was really nice, talking is cool, even if it doesn't all make sense, you're still doing something, connecting, just being there able to talk with her, seeing her, gosh where else is there? Then she would wander off, fall asleep and I would wait for her to wake again. I sat in the chair in the corner in the dark and I didn't stop anything, thoughts and feelings just went by.*

*Last night I was able to lift Betty to the bedside potty. Before that Big Mike would have to help. I couldn't hold her up at the same time, as soon as you lifted one side of her body the other side would fall over the other way. Last night it went fine so that's good.*

*After Betty fell asleep after 2:00 a.m. I went to bed. At 3:00 a.m. Big Mike came by my room and said he was going to Plano General Hospital emergency room and I fell back asleep.*

*I was woken by the phone at 4:00 a.m. It was Big Mike.*

*He'll just be Mike for the rest. He was in intensive care. He said he was very sick, with a fever 101°, dehydration and a very low blood count. He didn't sound good and he sounded scared. It was sad. He had to go and I fell back asleep. Eleanor woke me up at 7:00 a.m. knocking on the front door to be let in. I fell back asleep and woke at 9:30. "fell out of bed. Dragged a comb across my head. Found my way" sat with Betty and had a cup. Also ate some breakfast. She'd like barely nibble on a corner of toast. It was a nice morning. We live for this. Showered and went to Plano General at about 11:30 am.*

*Mike didn't look too good, he was very pale, his face didn't look right, didn't look healthy. When the nurse left his room to get blood I followed. I asked her if Mike's doctor had been contacted. She said no, who is his doctor? I'm not sure that she understood.*

*I said to her I thought his doctor may need to be consulted for treatment. She didn't know Mike is HIV+. I almost had to move my hand in front of her eyes, there was nothing there but an open oval mouth and big deer eyes. And then she seemed mad, she left everything she was doing and went somewhere with the news. Boy oh boy, what do you think? Someone should have said something. It doesn't seem right, people are dying. Shortly after talking to the nurse Tracy and I left, right when we got home the doctor from Plano General called and said they were going to transfer Mike to Baylor Hospital. Really. I guess there are two sides to this. Baylor has what Mike needs and on the other side, they don't want Mike here. People are dying.*

*Tracy and I came back to the hospital at 1:00 p.m. to be around with Mike and see him off for the transport. When we got there, Mike's temperature was 103°. Plano General couldn't transport him, he was too unstable, he had to stay. We didn't, we left back to Betty. Soon after the doctor called again, said Mike was going into surgery. We came back at about 6:00 p.m. Now it's 8:00 p.m. I'm sitting in the surgery waiting room. Before the surgery, the surgeon told us he was very concerned about Mike's chances, he said it was life-threatening. The surgeon said something had ruptured either in his stomach or in the large intestines or the appendix, they weren't sure till they go in. Somehow they know something has ruptured. It probably ruptured the other day when Mike grabbed his stomach and now he's bleeding or leaking internally. They feel the surgery should go okay but Mike will have a very difficult time with recovery fighting the infection.*

*This is the third time we've been at Plano General today and each time it's been f****** pounding and damaging. I'm tired and all day long we've been bombarded. Even the insurance company has been calling all day wanting hospice care for Betty. And here I am, sitting, finding relief and solace in a surgery waiting room.*

*Things are going on, and we have to stay up with it, it's fast.*

*It's 9:10 p.m. The surgeon just called over the waiting room phone and said Mike had gangrene perforated appendix. The appendix was removed, there is an infection or gangrene spreading through his body, there's an infection in his blood. He said Mike did well in surgery and is resting comfortably for the night. The surgeon said the chances are not in Mike's favor for his body to stop or destroy the infection and gangrene.*

*Same day, Monday, but now it's night. I made it home, like in a dream you 'get back home.' The house is very quiet, no one is here except Betty and I. A minute ago she was comfortable in her bed and then she said she had to go potty. I adorned the proper attire, and first lifted her back up off the bed to almost a sitting position. We sat there for a while and rested. Next I sat near her and with my arm over her shoulder I would raise Betty to her feet, rest and then move her around to the potty which she falls back onto. We did this and then she sat there on the pot and said she didn't have to go, we sort of sat there looking at each other, maybe*

*I was in the way, huh?*

*Now it's 11:00 p.m. of the night of the day that never started and hasn't ended.*

*I'm very comfortable lying in bed under nice clean sheets. Thank you to a very wonderful beautiful person, Eleanor.*

*The last word I heard from Tracy to Dan to Ally to Eleanor was that Mike was going to have a hard time surviving because of the gangrene and infections. He's already behind the 8 ball with how many bad infections are spreading and he's HIV+, with probably diminishing t-cells, making it even harder. I also heard that Linda and Laurie are either going to fly in tomorrow, or wait and see what happens next. I talked to Laurie earlier today about Mike and how the day was. She then spent part of the night in Andrew's treehouse drinking a bottle of wine and crying. Laurie is a trip. Like there's a small box and a big box in a room. In the small box is everything the other 5 of us did, in the big box is Laurie. But what Laurie did is not what defines her. Laurie is kindness, she is caring, loving, strong, it just came out wrong with the things that she did. I don't know. I'd pick Laurie.*

# Chapter 131

*Tuesday, August 3, 1993*

*It's been a busy day. There were times with Betty sitting quietly or talking. Although she doesn't talk much, she makes more sense. It's nice, the clowns, the girl, the men, have all gone. The walls of the room are painted off white. She may still mix up people, places or times, you can follow along and it is really nice to go where she goes.*

*I was running around with either Tracy or Ally, the other staying with Betty.*

*Mike is really sick, it happened so fast it was like bam, Bam, BAM, it's unreal.*

*How is that for someone who knows they are going to die soon, 1-2-3 months? What, where, with who, would you be doing if you were running out of time.*

*Mike is being laid off from his job on August 14th.*

*How is all of this going to fit together? Where is there enough of everyone in enough time? How is there enough heart for all of this to happen at once?*

*Betty is very quiet. There hasn't been too much communication, she can talk, it's just not very often. I sit with her or Tracy sits here, one of us is here. We comfort her with soft touches and soft voices. It seems to work, the vibes are good, and Betty is comfortable. It's nice.*

*Tracy's kids are here, they are so young, they're just babies and this is all going on around them. I wonder when they're older how they will remember Grandma Betty and how they remember this time. They will, they are very close to Grandma Betty and in their way they are involved. Every time they see Grandma, they hug her and they love her, baby love and she loves it.*

*There is another deal: I have an interview in Denver on Thursday, August 5, in two days. I have to do something, you think, I have to go, maybe not, I'll see.*

*I'd be right back. Tracy will move in while I'm gone, I don't know, I may be gone.*

# Chapter 132

*Saturday August 7th 1993*

*Awwww, we're about 4 miles from Texline, New Mexico. I felt terrible this morning. I'm sorry that during the short time I was in Denver I held on to the s*** that I did. I couldn't focus on what mattered. I apologize to everyone. I'm an ass. Again. Rats.*

*Maybe being away from the thick of things in Dallas allowed sadness, fear, frustrations to come busting out, it came out wrong, what I said, what I did, like Laurie does.*

*It was sad to leave Denver this morning. Sadness filled with regrets and love. Ryan and Tess are so lovely to be around. They're so joyful and happy. They're like the kids you see running, skipping, laughing in the sun. It was a nice couple of days. There was a party, a big dinner, lots of food, went to Cherry Creek. Ryan had the party for me on Thursday night. Tony and Steve were there, Bryson, Joanie, Linda, Aaron, Jenny and Ryan and Tess. I really enjoyed myself. I had a nice time with the kids, we enjoyed one another.*

*The trip was a trip and has sort of worked out fine to this point so far so good. We ended up staying in Denver till Saturday morning. Things are how they have been in Dallas.*

*It's weird the scene here in Denver and the scene in Dallas. They are very different and at the same time often the feelings are the same. In Denver I didn't hear crying, didn't see pain etched in faces, didn't feel death in any rooms. In Dallas I don't hear the robust laughter, don't see joy etched, but in both places Denver and Dallas I can feel the same thing. Love. I can see it, I can hear it, I can feel it where I am.*

*Dallas has been my life. There is only one way out.*

*We left Dallas for Denver last Wednesday at 9pm. I had an interview on Thursday. Leaving Dallas was a* *deal that was being put together as we were driving away. Katie came with me. We drove all night, long past midnight, past 3 a.m. and were going 85mph as we passed 5am Thursday morning. We drove all night through pounding rain, total darkness, no one out in the Panhandle except Katie and I. We drove right through our sleep and got to Denver at 10:00 a.m. Thursday for the 12:30 interview for a job that I didn't even f****** get!! F***! I almost thought I would get it, I was confused once about something I should have known but I have never known. I always get it mixed up, like I have to move my right hand to know my left, the 'i' before 'e' except after 'c', forget it, don't know it, I've tried. In the interview I messed up the other thing I can't keep straight. Fiction versus nonfiction. It's stupid, why would something real have 'non' before it? 'Non' makes things 'not', which makes nonfiction not real. It's not right. And I messed it up. I just have never been able to do these three things. Two of them are dumb.*

# Chapter 133



*Saturday night, August 7th, 1993*

*I got home from Denver tonight. It was good to see Betty. Being away you can see changes when you return. When you're always here, the changes and progression of HIV, you don't notice as much, it's subtle quiet changes. You leave for a couple days, then you see it. She was lying in the dark, her mouth was open, her eyes were closed and looked a bit sunken. Her breathing was heavy and when I held her she felt motionless, emotionless. Sort of blew me away and my thoughts went all over the place. I hugged her, I cried, I couldn't feel any response from her. Tracy didn't say anything, we were both thinking the same thing. We didn't think Betty was going to live through the night. It was like it was right there in the room with us. We sat in dim candlelight. We didn't move, didn't talk. Sat there in our own fear and sadness. The whole house was so quiet, not a sound, and it was dark, light wasn't allowed to be here. It was eerie there in the darkness.*

# Chapter 134

*Tuesday August 10th, 1993*

*The days are flying by to nowhere. I'm sitting here in Valley View Mall. It's very hard to tell what is going on with anything, and it's hard to do anything. I haven't written in a couple days, I don't know where the days are gone. It goes from one thing to another and even the transition between things, becomes a thing, it's all looped together. But it's not just flying through these things, there is constant engagement, deep connections being made. Maybe the past days we were in a rabbit's hole, around we would go in the dark from places to people and then end up back with Betty. It's crazy. I feel like a visitor to a different world. Look around, what do you see? I don't know, I don't know why we are at the mall, I have stopped walking, sat and am sipping a smoothie that makes me think of Ryan, someone from a different world.*

*Betty is doing well. She sleeps a lot. She seems comfortable, her face looks like there is calm inside her. There is not a lot of pain and she is able to come down to earth when she awakes. She's always thirsty. She will take small bites of toast during the day. It's not enough to sustain her, but it is working. She hasn't gotten to where she doesn't want to be.*

*The length of sleep time may vary, 1-2 hours at a time. When she wakes, she'll talk, she'll visit with who is there. She seems to follow along with what is going on around her. When she is awake, 2-3 times a day, Eleanor takes care of her. They'll get up, go to the bathroom. Eleanor cleans her up, changes her gowns, does her hair, moves Betty around, massages her muscles and her head. Things have been very nice. The darkness has become lighter.*

*Mike is still in the hospital and now they're saying he may get out Thursday or Friday, that's like in two days. I swear this would be miraculous if he comes home. I don't see how. There's no way that he can get out and live. He's been there for 10 days, they never really wanted him to stay. Doesn't seem right. Poor guy. He has gangrene in his body, a wild infection in his blood, I don't see how he and a couple hundred IVs of antibiotics are fighting this off. He does seem to be doing a little better and perking up a little, sometimes into his hyper self.*

*It's hard to say where I'm at with Mike. He was always a good guy. He enjoyed himself, was always in a good mood and happy.  He and Betty were good together and she was happy. But golly, what he did. Everyone has heard of AIDS and there are safe practices. He didn't control himself and transmitted HIV to Betty.*

*It's a deadly disease and Betty will die from it. It will kill her. If someone shot and killed her, what would it be?*

*I don't know.*

*Mike wants to get out of the hospital, he said he is*

*worried about Betty and he wants to come home. Ok. When he does we're all going to have to give up what has become pretty comfortable digs in this big house. It's almost amazing what accommodations death provides. It's been nice to have Tracy, there's lots of room, it's comfortable and Tracy being there is good. Tracy is a hard read. She can be the sweetest person and she can be harsh. For this situation and the things going on, she's the best, shares no emotions and nothing gets in her way, if it does she will rip it apart.*

*For the most part we don't talk much about Betty dying. I don't know, it seems to be okay, I guess you could talk about it, some of it is the same thing, words limit an experience, words define things too much. Or a place you are, where how you are, your actions, what you do, how you look, all convey as much as words. I don't need to ask Tracy how she is. I don't know, it's good to talk, we don't and we're good somewhere beyond words. Take me away.*

*I made a list of things I should do; bank accounts,*

*boxes, money, not enough money, the cemetery part, priest? probates, lawyer, personal property, insurance, hospital care, chaplains, and bills. It's hard to get into this stuff. And I talk to Harry, Linda, Laurie, Jeff and Ally. All at once everyone wants to know everything at the same time.*

# Chapter 135

*Thursday August 12th 1993*

*Betty is quiet, she's comfortable, she's beautiful. She's been in bed. Eleanor is here taking care of Betty. Eleanor keeps Betty comfortable, washes Betty, changes her. Eleanor provides whatever Betty needs. Maybe this is what Hospice Care is. It's been really nice, comfortable, there is not as much pain, she's not crawling on the bathroom floor. I don't know. The quality of interactions with Betty have been nice. Going calmly and comfortably.*

*Been working on the list. I've made some calls. Often it seems the person on the other end can't help me or doesn't want to. And maybe, possibly be impatient with a lot of things. Sometimes I find something out and it's not what I wanted, or needed or it's bad news. Other times it's just nothing there at all and it's a drag.*

*Most of what I say or write is coming from a place*

*inside of me where there's fear and sadness, anger and love, it's all mixed up. And it goes around and around, like this, watch my finger. It's crazy, there are times I'm messed up.*

*Trying to find out about taxes. I have to finish burial arrangements and we haven't even decided yet where to bury Betty. Not everyone, and to different degrees everyone understands some of the ideas or the plans. We've talked about some of the ideas or things that are happening, enough to make final decisions. Times up. The cemetery looks to be Evergreen Memorial Park in Evergreen Co, outside of Denver.*

# Chapter 136

*Friday August 13, 1993*

*Dim lights are everywhere, along with people who seem so quiet*

*Since Tuesday at the mall to this afternoon, many things were taken care of, settled or had lost their meaning.*

*One afternoon I went to the funeral home and the director said that everything was ready and I almost died.*

*One afternoon I was at Harry's office and there was no action.*

*Another afternoon I went to banks, an attorney's office and phone calls, many phone calls. All this stuff is associated with the same thing, you have to do this stuff. And it doesn't always flow easily together.*

*Aunt Barbara is here. She's a wonderful, beautiful spirit. Sisters being together bring a lot together for each other. Betty and Barbara grew up side by side, they are very similar. Barbara is how Betty would be without the constraints, freer spirit. They both check things off in their head, then knowing it is correct, they come out strongly and with passion. Passion adds to what you are doing. Wonderful feelings, love, desire, joy, all are there and enhanced by passion. Seems like passion enhances the same thing it is born from. If you love, you can make passion, you can create passion from being in love. And once you create passion from love, the passion will enhance your love.*

*And I think you can manifest passion, "this is really cool," I'm so glad I'm here with you" "You are so beautiful." Passion is the long hugs and flowers.*

# Chapter 137

*Saturday morning, August 14th, 1993*

*I'm having coffee with Betty, I don't know if she knows it. She's pretty relaxed and I'm trying to. She lies in bed, her eyes are closed, her hands are folded over her chest, her mouth is open, her breath are short heaves and then nothing, quietness.*

*The room is nice, soft music, flowing sheets and curtains, comfortable chairs around her bed. There are pictures and flowers. It's like she wants it.*

*When you walk in the room you can feel lots of life and death. Life and death in the same room, same body. You can't separate the two, they stay together till the end. I can see Betty's life all around her, I can feel an infinite love for her. And while you bask in life and love, death creeps in and I can see her dying.*

*There's acceptance. Caring and love in the air. Harry*

*with Betty and Betty for Harry. Aunt Barbara speaks more and more fondly of Uncle George, Laurie loves Ralph, Tracy finds love in the comfort of Dan and Jenny calls and I talk to her.*

*It makes sense that this situation we are in with Betty, there's love. Sparks of love come off of Betty, start a fire and create love elsewhere.*

*We want to love somebody and somebody to love us.*

*It is later, about 1:00 p.m., everyone has left for a while. Eleanor is washing Betty and everything is very quiet. Eleanor is wonderful, she does her job as a professional and then she has this incredible personal part that is so warm, gentle, kind and soft for Betty and for each of us. God sent Eleanor. The day has been nice and calm. Another lull, often followed by the magnificent.*

*Now it is even later, 9:15 p.m. I'm sitting in the den watching a movie with Goldie Hawn, Aunt Barbara,*

*Ben and Spike. The girls, Laurie, Ally and Tracy are sitting outside on the back porch. It is a nice night to be apart and alone. Linda may be coming in tonight.*

*Betty has been quiet in her bed most of the day, not too much movement. Eleanor takes wonderful care of Betty, makes sure she's hydrated and comfortable. Eleanor moves Betty, like exercise, to change clothing, clean sheets and takes her into the bathroom.*

# Chapter 138

*Sunday, August 15th, 1993*

*Mike was here. He was out on a pass, he said he wanted to see Betty.*

*Mikes not going to get out.*

*When I picked him up Plano General he was very anxious and uncomfortable. They had run a test, another CAT scan. They have found something on the liver and something on the stomach, and something on almost everything inside. They're hoping it is a lot of dead tissue. Mike was scared, he seemed angry. He swept through the house for 2 hours, distracted, irritated, never staying in one place, angry and indifferent to everyone around him, including Betty and this bothered me. Betty is most important.*

*When we got back to the hospital Mike was sitting on the edge of his deathbed and it hit him how he had just spent the last couple of hours at home and he started to cry. I don't think he is going to see Betty alive again and he wasn't even close to seeing that reality, blinded by his fear and anger. What we miss. It's so crazy. I've done it. Shit. I guess he could hardly help it, it is desperation, he's lost. While I was there the doctor stopped by and said that the test results necessitated surgery at 8:15 tomorrow morning. And you could feel this tremendous, absolutely tremendous monster rise up wielding its wrath. Then it was very quiet, each of us staring at the floor. Wondering.*

# Chapter 139

*Monday, August 16, 1993*

*So now it's today. Ally and Tracy were at Plano General at 6:30 a.m. I got there about 7:30 and I left a couple hours later at 9:30.*

*Mike was still in surgery. At 11:30 a.m. 5 hours later, Tracy called from the hospital. Mike has lymphoma cancer all over the inside of his body. He has seven cancerous tumors on his liver, and there are tumors on his other organs. The surgeon said he was very sorry but when they saw the spread and extent of the cancer in Mike all they could do was to sew him back up. There is nothing in this world that will save Mike. Nothing they could do can stop the infections and cancer. It's over. Almost right when it started, it's going to end. Can you believe that? I can't. We've done pretty well with the incredible happening around us, then there is the unbelievable and inconceivable.*

*We're not talking about that "fuck, I can't believe that happened" we're talking about unbelievable beyond that. Never a thought that this would happen. I'm sitting here, upside down on the ceiling and I'm looking around and I just can't believe what I see.*

*And you know, there's much worse. Many people suffer the unimaginable. There's horror. It seems you bring horror into anything and it's way worse, 10x, 100x. Horror and fear, horror and pain, horror and death. Oh my God bless them. We've touched it.*

*How it is now, I like how Betty is dying. I think she does too. It's what she's wanted. She's gently fading off to somewhere.*

*I'm tired, I can't be how I am for long. I wish again upon a falling star, someone to love me, someone close to me.*

*Love is there, it's real, really happens. Thank God for love.*

# Chapter 140

*It's later Monday*

*We just finished eating Chinese food, Aunt Barbara, Linda, Laurie and I. Now we are stuffed, lying around sort of watching Lonesome Dove? It seems like it would be a good movie. Everyone is just sitting, resting and thinking about what we just did.*

*We moved a lot of Betty's stuff out of the house over to Ally's house. Mike had called and said his mom is in town today and tomorrow and this set something in motion, something where we wanted to have Betty's personal stuff. We weren't interested in their stuff, just Betty's. Like everything she collects, her knick knacks and her pictures, all the things she had for every holiday, her jewelry. I don't know, you just figure it out. It was weird, it was hard, it was sad and it was probably close to the right thing to do. Everyone sort of quietly moved things, trying not to disturb anything that would draw our attention to what we were doing in real life. It was weird closing things up, is this how it is done? There were decisions that had to be made. The decisions just kept popping up in each room where someone was looking at stuff. Mike and Betty's life. Like raindrops on a puddle, 'ping' there it is, you have to respond fast, it's quickly gone and then another drop 'ping', "What about this Santa, Betty bought it at Sanger-Harris?" There were a lot of things to go through, many meant something and became treasures that each time they're taken out, they will touch your heart.*

*It was good what we did. Pretty sure the house is in Mike's name and like Betty would say "you never know what people may do in a situation." Mike won't be back. Better to do now while we are here and other survivors are not. So, probably being very fair and honest we took stuff, Betty's.*

# Chapter 141

*Tuesday, August 17, 1993*

*It's morning, everything is quiet.*

*I'm sitting bedside with Betty, her eyes half closed.*

*18-4, 18-3, 15-4, 18-4, 17-3,*

*This is Betty's breathing pattern, 18 seconds with no breath and then four short desperate gasps for air, then 18 seconds, nothing, three gasps and it continues. I count the seconds off on the IV clock. For 18 seconds there's not a sound, Betty lays there, she does not move then she is jolted back to life gasping for air. It's so unreal. Life and death are so close to each other, I wonder how close for each of us. I wonder how many times in a lifetime death is in the same room with us, the same car, same street or alley. How often are we that close?*

*Betty's bedroom is so nice. While we were taking*

*Later*

*All around things go faster and faster.*

*Linda not knowing what to do, trying to decide what may matter, does she stay or go. Laurie every once in a while is quieted by the immenseness of what is going on.*

*Aunt Barbara going home and realizing how*

*wonderful and beautiful it has been.*

*There's a poem, "Digging Worms" by Robert Bly.*

*And we all try to balance the final delicate moments of Betty's life in the greatness of love. Betty.*

# Chapter 142

*Thursday, August 19th, 1993*

*It is 12:10 p.m., exactly.*

*It feels as if time has not moved and it is the darkest of hours all the time.*

*I can't do anything.*

*Last night stops me dead, a part of me died. I saw it, I touched it, felt it, tentacles of it were in the room all around. Everything was dark except for a thin light that would shoot out from the lamp, out from the bathroom or up from the floor. The light was there to guide us.*

*Laurie and I walked into Betty's room to kiss her good night. We're standing in the clear of the light and Betty was there. She had made a huge catastrophic mess in her bed.*

*It seemed to cover everything, draped over everything, like horror. It was on Betty's body, her nightgown, it covered the sheets, the bed, the floor, everything was covered with her vomit and waste. She was almost seated up in the bed, vile and vomit was still seeping out of her mouth, her hands held up cupping vomit and she was crying. It was the most she's been alive for the last days.*

*The smell was overwhelming, it seemed to be alive, its presence was more than anything else in the room. It was so hard to breathe, you didn't want to.*

*Everything that could in this situation was happening and it was all against you, and you couldn't stop it.*

*There was pain, fear and death that you could touch, it was so real. We were scared of everything. Petrified, at first we couldn't move, we didn't know what to do, where to walk, where to go, where to start. Then we were startled into moving, at first just barely, we couldn't figure out what to do first.*

*I don't know how conscious we were, it hurt too much to know what you were doing.*

*We cut Betty's night gown off from the back to avoid lifting it over her head. We rolled Betty back and forth and back and forth to clean her body, she would moan from pain every time we moved her. It was the only sound in the room, deep heavy moans. Her body was like holding jello, it had lost its shape and its form. Her muscles and bones provided no structure.*

*Laurie cleaned everything. She cleaned Betty's body, all the crevices that were covered with all this s***.*

*We were very tender. I held Betty up while Laurie washed. On Betty's face were teardrops. She knew what was going on, it made her cry that we were there. She had tears in her eyes and one by one they would roll down her face. The tears never left the whole time we were cleaning her up. Betty hated that this happened and if she could have talked she would have screamed at the top of her voice, "Stop it."*

*It was unbelievable. All the while we were cleaning up, we didn't say anything, no words.*

*When we were finished we sat in the dark on the back porch, nothing said. After a bit we went back to Betty's room to kiss her good night. She was lying in bed, gagging, green vial, vomit coming out of her mouth, and this wonderful beautiful child of God was crying out. She had made another mess in her bed. It was all there again. This time I could feel everything fleeing my body, not wanting to be here again. There was still love, there was no hesitation, we cut her nightgown, removed the sheets, rolled her back and forth to clean her body, to dress her and to get new sheets on her bed. I'd whisper in her ear to calm her tears, telling her that it was going to be alright. We're passing the time Betty, I'm sorry. It's that it is so unimaginable.*

*After three hours Betty was asleep in her room. Laurie and I are in a place deep inside ourselves. It's so dark. It's a place I don't really want to be, a place now awaken will never go away. Oh I can't believe this.*

# Chapter 143

*Friday, August 20th, 1993*

*It's the morning*

*A constant torment inside my head from yesterday.*

*I don't know how alive I am.*

*I have to do something.*

*I don't know what.*

*Oh my God.*

*It's the afternoon*

*Dale said there'd be a sign and once Betty passed that sign she can't come back.*

*I heard the most beautiful thing. Eleanor said she was sent here to keep Betty beautiful for all the kids and she does so relentlessly with love.*

# **Chapter 144**

*Saturday, August 21st 1993*

*There are people here.*

*Geez, I don't know, the last couple of days, I was so inside myself, it was weird, couldn't get out.*

*Now it's Saturday. I'm sitting in the backyard. I feel anxious about things, uneasy about stuff. I wish a lot of the stuff would go back down or go away but if it does it takes Betty with it.*

*Letting go, keeps coming back. The thought that if we keep wanting to hold on to Betty then it's not allowing her to go. I don't need to let her go after all, and I'm not going to let go. I'm holding on to it forever. In my head, I'm holding on to memories, in my heart I'm holding onto love. I'm not letting Betty go.*

*Laurie left this morning. Laurie spends many moments in her grandeur. Everything that is the very best of*

*Laurie often came out while she was here. Laurie was sincere, loving and thoughtful. She used her time with Betty like it was blessed. It benefited both of them. Laurie spent quiet time with Betty, she talked to Betty. Laurie would massage Betty with lotions of beautiful smelling flowers. It was really good that Betty and Laurie had time together, it took care of anything between them. You could see it meant a lot to Betty.*

*The other night Laurie was out of this world, she was incredible, she rose up two times herself. She earned a good life.*

*She wanted to leave but it was very hard for her to. Something is moving her away, and she would wonder why, she wouldn't know why she was leaving.*

*There's a bird chirping loudly, they want me to move so that they can eat.*

*Now no one is here, everyone has left. Here I am.*

*Saturday evening*

*Jeff came to town today. He's different from something. It was good to see him. It was more of a light visit and a few solemn moments. Jeff doesn't go there in public. He came with another girlfriend, Paulette. It seemed his part in the relationship with Paulette as genuine that I've seen him with before. He has a certain level of energy that sometimes is wielded awkwardly around other people. I don't know, we've always gotten along despite being different.*

*It is hard to say about Betty. I sat with her this morning. Her comfort level is fair, something is causing her discomfort, her mental being is more than nothing. Hearing is not heard by anyone inside her. Physically she can't move her head, her lips quiver, her shoulders quicker, her whole body quivers from inside her. She tries to raise her arm and it moves nowhere from her side. It is hard to see and hard to be. There's comfort, and even that is being hard to maintain. There's a slight breeze blowing the chime.*

# Chapter 145

*Monday morning, August 23rd, 1993*

*So far this morning things are pretty good. Jeff left. Tracy and her kids are moving into Big Mike's room after school today. It'll be nice to have them around.*

*We had a different nurse yesterday over the weekend. The nurse was surprised that Betty in her condition was alive. I don't understand that, there are still times that Betty has. The nurse spent most of the day getting ready for something because Betty was going to die very soon any minute. During the past 3 weeks Betty has lived through many people and different nurses all of whom have said that Betty was going to die at any time and we have too, so many times. When you add all these minutes up, Betty has died everyday during the past 3 weeks and on one day she died twice. She faces death everyday. She wakes up to it, spends a day with it, bids good night to it, every single day.*

*Betty's room is beginning to rival the sanctuary of the backyard. There's music, the robust smell of flowers and candles. It's nice, couldn't be better.*

# Chapter 146

*Monday night*

*I'm sitting on the floor in the dark in Betty's room. It's almost midnight, almost Tuesday morning. Tracy is back in bed.*

*You are only on your way, and all this happens.*

*I'm sitting on the floor and I can't move. I'm sitting with a nurse I can't see, who Tracy has cussed out, it was more of a scream from Tracy, I heard it. A scream filled with fear and sadness. The nurse and I are sitting quietly in the darkness waiting for a pharmacist to deliver a new pump with Dilaudid in it. Dilaudid is fucking crazy. Betty's blood came out of her body, up through the line into the IV pump and filled the hanging bag of Dilaudid with blood. This happened 2 hours ago after an incredibly long day.*

*Tracy and I have spent the last 2 hours asking each*

*other what should we do? After we had done everything there was to do, we had to know what to do now. You can't budge from what you have to do. Betty's temperature has been 102' all day and up to 104'. Betty's hands turned blue during the day, they were real life blue, freaked me out for what seemed like hours but will probably be forever. It's so dark and quiet. It's unreal. The pharmacist is here, narcotics delivery.*

*I have to do something.*

*I have to get out of my head and come from the heart*

*I don't know how to do it.*

# Chapter 147

*Tuesday August 24th, 1993*

*It's the afternoon. I'm sitting in almost complete quietness. Even things that make noise are silent. There's a white buzzing hum is all I can hear.*

*It's 120 p.m. Tracy went to get groceries and pick up the kids. Eleanor is with Betty, keeping her cool and comfortable. Her temperature has been between 102 and 104°.*

*I'm sorry Betty.*

*There are times when she seems almost comatose. The comfort measures are harder to maintain. There are infections and pain in parts of her body. The fever rises because her body is fighting beyond its normal state. And then her pulse quickens, her heart beating quickly to keep her alive. The drugs take her to the moon, Dilaudid and every 3 hours a shot of Valium.*

*I see her, I can hear her breaths, and that is all.*

*How long can she be like this? Her heart is strong, her lungs, her liver, her body organs are all functioning well. She can remain like this, I don't know how she will die like this.*

*People say something needs to be done. What are they talking about? Do they have any idea?*

*Betty had said, "please don't let this happen."*

*Maybe I'm the wrong person.*

*I stopped by church yesterday. Prayed for Betty. Prayed for strength. Send the light.*

*I'm going to be with her tonight.*

# Chapter 148

*Wednesday, August 25th, 1993*

*Dear Betty,*

*The night is over. I thought it would go on forever.*

*I'm in your room. So hard to say anything.*

*I can't believe you're not in your room. I can't believe you're not anywhere. I can't believe you're not here.*

*Last night. I can see you all the time, your heart was heaving, your temperature was 106 °. All night you were burning up. Things were not going well.*

*Betty, are you okay?*

*Did you know what was happening?*

*I love you Betty*

*I didn't know what to do. I never knew how to do it.*

*It was dark. A sliver of light, a candlelight.*

*It was so quiet.*

*The only sound, your breathing, a few short breaths and then very quiet. The room felt empty.*

*I could feel your heart pounding.*

*It was 4:49 when you died. It didn't take long and the minute has lasted forever.*

*I'm sorry Betty, I hope it was all right.*

*It seemed like it was. You hardly moved, you didn't seem to notice or feel anything, like it just happened. Your breathing was the same till it wasn't anymore. Your pillow held your last breath.*

*Betty, it was very gentle and peaceful. You died very softly, the way you wanted.*

*I love you.*

*Wayne*

# Chapter 149

*Wednesday, August 25th, 1993*

*Hello Betty,*

*Thought you might want to know about the day. It's into the night now.*

*The day was very sad, people were terribly saddened to hear about your death.*

*Everyone lost so much.*

*Linda flew in right away. She was terribly upset and alone in Denver. She had no idea what to do. She's better now that she is here.*

*I haven't spoken with Laurie. I left a message, she won't respond. We will see her soon. Laurie was a sweetheart while she was here. She did not miss a beat giving everything she had to comfort you. It all created an immeasurable amount of love that she always had for you. I missed her when she left.*

*Jeff is here, drove in about 7:00 this evening. He was worried about not being able to find his 17 year old suit he wore at one of his weddings. He's glad to be here, he helps Ally and Tracy. They both hang on to him for something, they think he's so wonderful.*

*I'm here.*

*Ally has been here the whole day. She spent time with you this morning.*

*You laid in your bed for a couple hours. It was good. Ally cries. She doesn't share her feelings, things don't come out of Ally. She was horrified when attendants wheeled you out of the bedroom and out of the house.*

*Tracy on the outside is doing pretty well. She went into your room this morning. She said your name. Her thoughts are that you died quietly, peacefully, no more pain, no more suffering. Tracy was so persistent over the year that you never suffer. That's all she wanted.*

*Harry had just arrived in Brazil, only Harry would be in Brazil. As you always said he was out of town for the big things. A couple people said that he was near hysterics when he heard of your death. He loved you.*

*Eleanor was wonderful and beautiful and provided so much comfort. She's a lot like you, working so hard for others, for her kids, her grandkids, always worried about them, wanting nothing to harm them or scare them. They are everything to her and her to them and you to us. Eleanor was here all day, she did everything. She said we had affected her life.*

*Dale came by. Betty, you were his sweetheart, you left a very special place in his heart. He is very touched by you. He's a good person. His hugs are comforting.*

*Tina came by, she brought lots of food for everyone. You two were very good friends, two nurses, comrades at the hospital.*

*Aunt Barbara is coming back into town tomorrow*

*afternoon. She's wonderful.*

*Jenny and Ryan and Tess are coming in this morning. Every night I talked to Ryan she always said "tell Grandma I love her."*

*Betty it's over.*

*I called out to you, did you hear me?*

*I pray and hope that everything is okay with you.*

*I love you.*

*You were everything.*

*Lots of love*

*Wayne*